YORK NOTES

The Franklin's Prologue and Tale

Geoffrey Chaucer

Note by J. A. Tasioulas

 Longman   York Press

J. A. Tasioulas is hereby identified as author of this work in accordance with
Section 77 of the Copyright, Designs and Patents Act 1988

YORK PRESS
322 Old Brompton Road, London SW5 9JH

PEARSON EDUCATION LIMITED
Edinburgh Gate, Harlow,
Essex CM20 2JE, United Kingdom
Associated companies, branches and representatives throughout the world

First published 2000

ISBN 0-582-41469-5

Designed by Vicki Pacey
Phototypeset by Gem Graphics, Trenance, Mawgan Porth, Cornwall
Colour reproduction and film output by Spectrum Colour
Produced by Addison Wesley Longman China Limited, Hong Kong

Contents

PART THREE

CRITICAL APPROACHES

PART FOUR

EXTENDED COMMENTARIES

PART FIVE

BACKGROUND

PART ONE

INTRODUCTION

HOW TO STUDY A NARRATIVE POEM

Studying a narrative poem on your own requires self-discipline and a carefully thought-out work plan in order to be effective.

- You will need to read the poem more than once. Start by reading it quickly for pleasure, then read it slowly and thoroughly.
- Look up all the words which you do not know. Some may have more than one meaning, so note them.
- On your second reading make detailed notes on the plot, characters and themes. Further readings will generate new ideas.
- Think about how the poem is narrated. From whose point of view are the events described? Does your response to the narrator change at all in the course of the poem?
- The main character is the narrator, but what about the others? Do they develop? Do you only ever see them from the narrator's point of view?
- Identify what styles of language are used in the poem.
- Assess what the main arguments are in the poem. Who are the narrator's main opponents? Are their views ever fairly presented?
- Are words, images or incidents repeated so as to give the work a pattern? Do such patterns help you to understand the poem's themes?
- What is the effect of the poem's ending? Is the action completed and closed, or left incomplete and open?
- Does the poem present a world or point of view of which you are meant to approve?
- Cite exact sources for all quotations. Wherever possible find your own examples to back up your opinions.
- Always express your ideas in your own words.

This York Note offers an introduction to *The Franklin's Tale* and cannot substitute for close reading of the text and the study of secondary sources.

No other pilgrim in *The Canterbury Tales* has caused as much debate as Chaucer's Franklin. This ruddy-faced country gentleman is famed for his hospitality. Every kind of delicacy is to be found in his house – pies, fish, partridges, meat and all sorts of rich sauces. He goes so far that the great folding table of the medieval country house is never put away. This is good living on a grand scale. There is no local office that he has not held, no dish that he has not served. 'Santa Claus' some critics call him, praising his generosity and good disposition. However, to others he is a monster, a gluttonous upstart clawing his way up the social ladder. His supporters and detractors battle it out over a portrait that shows Chaucer's delicately **ambiguous** style at its best.

Debate continues over *The Franklin's Tale*. It is allegedly a pretty **romance** but it shakes medieval beliefs to their core. The very foundations of medieval marriage are questioned and the conventions of romantic love held up to scrutiny. The Middle Ages demanded that a wife be subordinate to her husband but what would happen if there were equality in marriage? Is a relationship based on equality even possible? What is it that makes a good marriage? These are some of the questions raised by *The Franklin's Prologue and Tale*. To many readers it has seemed like a triumph of equality over the social situation, an ideal relationship after so many accounts of bad marriages in *The Canterbury Tales*. Others, however, feel that the possibility of change is only raised in order to show what terrible things happen when women are allowed too much freedom and power.

It is not, however, just a tale about marriage. It also raises issues about what it really means to be 'noble'. Is it merely a matter of birth or is everyone capable of noble acts? In a period of great social change, Chaucer examines the vows that hold medieval society together, questioning their nature and asking if it is a rational way to live. It is a tale of magic and rash promises, love and despair, but its concerns are fundamental to the real world. This rosy-cheeked Franklin has taken a traditional romance, almost a fairy story, and has used it to ask serious questions about male domination in marriage, the swearing of feudal oaths and the nature of true gentility. What the reader must decide, however, is whether the tale presents a brave new world of social and sexual equality, or raises these issues only to show what disasters occur when people do not know their rightful place.

PART TWO

COMMENTARIES

The Franklin's Prologue and Tale *is one of the twenty-four stories that make up* The Canterbury Tales. *This work was left unfinished by Chaucer when he died and the order in which he intended the tales to be read is not clear. We do know that the Franklin should follow* The Squire's Tale, *a story of kings and princesses, magical horses and talking birds, but it is not clear who should come after the Franklin. Chaucer wrote before the invention of printing and his work therefore survives in manuscripts that would have been copied out by hand.*

The standard edition of the complete works of Chaucer is: Larry D. Benson, ed., The Riverside Chaucer, *Houghton Mifflin, 1987. A single edition of the text can be found in A.C. Spearing, ed.,* The Franklin's Prologue & Tale, *Cambridge University Press, 1966, which is the text used in compiling this Note.*

SYNOPSIS

A group of pilgrims on their way to Canterbury are passing the time on their journey by telling one another stories. Many have already told their tales and a young Squire has just been recounting a marvellous adventure involving magical horses and talking birds when he is interrupted by a Franklin, a country gentleman with a fondness for the good life and a liking for tales of knights and ladies. He praises the Squire, bemoans the lifestyle of his own son, muses on the need for gentility and is eventually told to get on with it by the Host, who demands that the Franklin tell his own story. The Franklin claims he is an unlearned man but proceeds to tell a lofty tale of love and honour.

Once upon a time in Brittany, a knight falls in love with a beautiful and noble lady. He begs her to take pity upon his suffering, offering himself as her humble servant, until she is finally moved by his devotion and agrees to be his wife. The knight, whose name is Arveragus, promises the lady, whose name is Dorigen, that he will continue to serve her in all things, asking only that, for the sake of his reputation, he should be her master in name. Dorigen agrees to this and in turn promises to be his faithful wife.

About a year after their wedding, Arveragus tells his wife that he must go and seek adventure in England. Dorigen is devastated and weeps constantly, faints continually and refuses to eat. Her friends try to comfort her and take her walking on the cliffs but Dorigen will not be consoled. Watching the boats sailing on the sea below, she catches sight of the dangerous rocks along the coastline and is horrified at the threat they pose to the ships. How can God allow such fiendish rocks to exist when they can bring nothing but harm to his creatures? Her friends see that the rocks are disturbing her and they take her elsewhere, attempting to divert her with games and dancing.

At one such dance, when Dorigen stands alone in the garden, still pining for her husband, she is approached by Aurelius, a neighbour and a young man of good reputation. He has been secretly in love with Dorigen for more than two years but has never dared tell anyone, revealing his love only in the songs and poems he composes. Now, however, he can conceal his feelings no longer and declares to Dorigen that he is in love with her. Dorigen's response is sharp and direct: she has no intention of being unfaithful to her husband, and that's her final answer. However, the 'finality' of her answer is undermined as she jokingly adds that there is one thing Aurelius could do that would win her love: if he were to remove all the threatening rocks in the sea, then she would indeed love him. Aurelius goes home despondent, realising the impossibility of the task. Meanwhile, Arveragus returns home from England to Dorigen's delight, and the two of them live joyfully together once more.

Two years pass, and Aurelius is still tormented by his feelings but can confide in no-one except his brother. His brother is deeply grieved to see him suffer and thinks of a plan to help him. He remembers that when he was a student he had seen a book of natural magic belonging to one of his friends. Some such magic or illusion could surely deal with the little matter of the rocks. Aurelius is delighted at the plan and the two leave immediately for the university. Just outside the town, they are greeted by a man who miraculously knows who they are and the nature of their business. He takes them to his home and conjures all sorts of wonders, including a vision of Aurelius dancing with Dorigen. The men discuss their problem and the clerk agrees to make the rocks disappear for 1,000 pounds in gold.

The clerk works night and day until he accomplishes his task. Aurelius is overjoyed and immediately seeks out Dorigen to tell her that the rocks have gone and to remind her of her promise. Dorigen stands as though turned to stone, all the blood drained from her face. She makes her way home with difficulty and spends two days weeping and fainting, bemoaning her fate. It seems to her that she has no honourable choice left except suicide and she recalls all the women of history who chose death over sexual dishonour. Arveragus has been away briefly but now returns home and is met by the grief-stricken Dorigen who tells him what she has done. 'Is this all, Dorigen?' he asks. He tells her that she must keep her promise, for 'Truth is the highest thing that one can keep'. However, he then bursts into tears and makes her swear that she will tell no-one else what she has done.

Aurelius has been watching the house and sees Dorigen leave. He accosts her in the busiest street in town to ask where she is going and is told that she was on her way to keep her promise to him, as her husband commanded. Aurelius is astonished and feels pity both for the weeping Dorigen and for the honourable Arveragus. He tells her that he does not wish to come between them and that she should return to her husband at once, observing that a squire like himself is as capable of a noble deed as a knight like Arveragus. Dorigen thanks him on her knees and returns home immediately with the good news.

It is not, however, such good news for Aurelius who has not only given up the woman he loves but is seriously in debt. He only has about half the amount he owes the clerk and wonders if he will agree to take the rest in instalments. The clerk is perplexed: hasn't he made the rocks disappear and hasn't Dorigen kept her word? Aurelius explains about the pity he felt for Dorigen and the generous sense of honour displayed by her husband in making her keep her promise. Impressed by the noble behaviour shown on all sides, the clerk declares that he will not be outdone in generosity and releases Aurelius from his debt. All that remains is for the Franklin to ask one last question: who was the most generous of them all?

General Prologue lines 333–62

The Franklin is a warm, hospitable landowner

Each of Chaucer's pilgrims is described in turn in the *General Prologue* at the beginning of *The Canterbury Tales*.

The Franklin is first seen riding along on the pilgrimage in the company of the Sergeant of the Law, a high-ranking lawyer. He himself is a country gentleman who has held many prominent positions in the shire: he has been a justice of the peace, a member of parliament, a sheriff and an auditor. His status and wealth are confirmed by the description of his household, where a large table always stands laden with all the best food of the season. The Franklin delights in this good living. With his rosy cheeks and white hair and beard he looks like a daisy, beaming at the world around him.

> The Franklin's portrait differs from those of most of the other pilgrims in that very little of it is actually a direct description of the Franklin. The first line establishes that he is travelling along with the Sergeant of the Law, certainly a wealthy and important man, but one whose own portrait has traditionally been viewed as **satiric**. This, of course, is not a direct criticism of the Franklin, except insofar as one is judged by the company one keeps. His sanguine temperament and daisy-like appearance take up the next two lines, both of which have positive associations in the Middle Ages, sanguinity being regarded as a healthy constitution and the daisy being a well-loved, if not very exciting, flower. However, there then follows a long account of the Franklin's eating habits and the sort of fare that was always on offer in his house. The sheer length of this description, together with the loving details of partridges being fattened in cages and pike being bred in the ponds, has led to accusations of gluttony being made against the Franklin, and there is admittedly a good deal of conspicuous consumption in this portrait. The Franklin may have held many distinguished offices but the description of these occupies only three lines as opposed to the twenty-one lines of eating and drinking that appear to be the Franklin's main concern. Add to this the observation that he was 'a very son' of the pleasure-loving philosopher Epicurus, and

the Franklin could find himself condemned as a gluttonous and decadent man with no concern for anything except his own belly. And yet, such a view would ignore much of the evidence and fail to capture the tone and spirit of the passage. The Franklin may be Epicurean in his habits but he is also compared to St Julian, the patron saint of hospitality. If there is a love of pleasure in this portrait it is also the love of pleasure shared, and there is a good deal of warmth in the description of this daisy-faced landowner. He is excessive in his desire for good living but it is good country fare nevertheless. His dagger and purse mark him out as a gentleman, but even here we cannot get away from the food imagery as his wallet is declared to be 'as white as morning milk'. Still, there are worse things for a purse to be, and worse things a man could be than a 'worthy' franklin.

berd beard

dayesye daisy

complexioun temperament

sangwin sanguine

Wel loved ... wyn he loved to have bread soaked in wine for breakfast

delit pleasure

wone custom

Epicurus owene sone the son of Epicurus himself. The ancient Greek philosopher Epicurus argued that pleasure was the beginning and end of a proper way of life. In his opinion, one could not live pleasurably without also living wisely and righteously, but he later came to be associated with carefree living and hedonism

pleyn delit pure pleasure

verray felicitee parfit true and perfect happiness

An housholdere ... he he was the head of a household, and a great one at that

breed bread

after oon of the same high quality

envined stocked with wine

bake mete freshly baked pies

flessh meat

snewed snowed

THE PORTRAIT OF THE FRANKLIN: GENERAL PROLOGUE continued

mete food

deyntees delicacies

koude thinke could imagine

After the ... yeer according to the various seasons of the year

soper supper

partrich partridge

muwe cage

breem bream

luce pike

stuwe fish pond

Wo in trouble

but if unless

Poynaunt piquant

sharp tasty

geere utensils

His table ... alway his table always stood ready in his hall

At sessiouns ... sire he presided at court sessions

Ful ofte ... shire he was a member of parliament many times

anlaas dagger

gipser purse

Heeng hung

girdel belt

morne morning

shirreve sheriff

contour auditor

vavasour landholder

THE PROLOGUE OF THE FRANKLIN'S TALE

LINES 37–56   **The Franklin says he will tell an old story but apologises in advance for his lack of learning**

After a discussion with the Landlord (lines 1–36), the Franklin declares that he will tell a Breton **lai** but wants to point out that he is a plain-speaking man, rough and unlearned and not at all skilled in the art of public speaking. He says that he has never been inspired by the eloquent muses on Mount Parnassus, has never studied Cicero, and knows nothing at all about the embellishments of **rhetoric**.

The Franklin begins by begging the company to forgive his plain style of talking, saying that he knows nothing about the art of public speaking. However, this disclaimer is not meant to be taken seriously: apologising for one's lack of rhetorical skill is itself a rhetorical device intended to gain the sympathy of the audience. Similarly, for a man who says he is unlearned, he is very familiar with classical names such as Cicero and Parnassus. Despite his claims, the Franklin's *Prologue* is highly rhetorical. It is not a virtuoso performance but it immediately establishes the Franklin as a man of lofty sympathies, if not pretensions. It also raises one of the key themes of the tale – truth and illusion – for the Franklin's very first action is to create an image of himself that is not true. However, as the tale will show, truth is a complicated matter, and the Franklin may, in fact, come closest to the truth when he thinks he is at his most rhetorical. His claim to be an uneducated man is intended to be the modest pose of a great public speaker, but the illusory image may be far closer to reality than the Franklin guesses. We have not yet reached *The Franklin's Tale*, and already issues of truth, image and self-perception have been raised.

37 **gentil** noble

  hir their

38 **layes** lais, short romances

39 **Rimeyed in ... tonge** composed in the original language of the Bretons

40 **songe** sang

41 **redden hem** read them

  plesaunce pleasure

42 **oon** one

44 **burel** plain

46 **rude** rough

47 **rethorik** rhetoric, the art of public speaking

  certeyn certainly

48 **Thing that ... pleyn** anything I say has to be plain and simple

49 **sleep** slept

49 **Mount of Pernaso** Mount Parnassus, home of the muses who governed art and literature

50 **Marcus Tullius Scithero** Cicero, Roman author of a great treatise on rhetoric

51 **Colours** rhetorical embellishments

52 **swiche** such

mede meadow

53 **peynte** paint

54 **queynte** unfamiliar

55 **My spirit ... mateere** my brain understands nothing of these things

56 **list** like

heere hear

The Franklin's Tale

Lines 57–88   A knight falls in love with a beautiful lady and asks her to be his wife

Once upon a time in Armorica, a knight falls in love with a beautiful and noble lady. He scarcely dares hope that she will love him in return but, nevertheless, performs chivalric deeds for her sake and tells her of his suffering. The lady is moved by this noble knight's devotion, and particularly by his submissiveness. Finally, she takes pity on him and agrees to become his wife. The knight promises to obey her in all things but asks that it should seem to the world as though he is the one in control. The lady agrees and in return promises to be his humble and true wife.

The Franklin's Tale is unusual in that it begins where most other romances leave off, with the marriage of the knight and lady. Neither character is named at this point, what we have instead are the stereotypical characters of courtly love poetry: a man who adores a noble lady from afar, humbly enduring her disdain until the woman finally condescends to grant him her love. This tale, however, is going to go beyond the stereotypes and the 'happy-ever-afters' and examine the nature of marriage. The curtain, therefore, rises on this happy ending and takes a good look at the lovers' promises that are usually rushed over in a mad dash to the finish. Surprisingly, our stereotypical knight is making a far from customary marriage vow, promising that he will obey his wife and honour her 'as any lovere to his lady shal' (line 78). The lady takes this as a sign of his 'gentillesse' (line 82) and in her turn pledges her 'trouthe' (line 87) that she will be his faithful wife. These are two of the key words in the tale and the importance of *trouthe* and the true nature of *gentillesse* will be revealed in the course of the narrative. It is a blissful picture in many ways but there are still one or two worrying aspects. In the very act of accepting her equality, the lady still sees herself as subordinate, thanking her husband for granting her 'so large a reine' (line 83), a **metaphor** which presents her as a tethered animal. Similarly, while the knight is happy to give authority to his wife, he still wants it to seem to the world as though he is the dominant partner. Their marriage is, therefore, bound up in illusion from the beginning. It may sound ideal but their words may cover a less beguiling reality. As the opening line of the tale shows, the exotic Armorica is in the end just plain old Brittany.

57   **Armorik**   Armorica
     Britaine   Brittany
58   **dide his paine**   took great trouble
59   **in his beste wise**   as best he could
60   **emprise**   chivalric exploit
61   **for his lady wroghte**   performed for his lady
     er   before
62   **oon the faireste under sonne**   the most beautiful on earth
63   **And eek … kinrede**   and she was also of such noble lineage
64   **wel unnethes**   scarcely
     dorste   dares
65   **peyne**   suffering
66   **for his worthinesse**   on account of his excellence
67   **namely**   especially
     meke obeisaunce   meek submissiveness
68   **Hath swich … penaunce**   took such pity on his suffering
69   **prively**   privately
     fil of his accord   came to an agreement with him
71   **swich**   such

71 **han** have

hir their

72 **And for … lives** and in order to make their lives even happier

73 **swoor hire** promised her

75–6 **Ne sholde …jalousie** would not assume the dominant role against her will, nor display any jealousy

79–80 **Save that … degree** except, in order not to be shamed as her husband, he wished to be her sovereign lord in name

81 **humblesse** humility

82 **sith** since

gentillesse courtesy

83 **profre** offer

so large a reine so loose a rein (i.e. such freedom)

84–5 **Ne wolde …stryf** may God never allow there to be any disagreement or argument between us through any fault of mine

87 **trouthe** promise

breste burst

LINES 89–118   The Franklin digresses on the need for freedom and tolerance in a relationship

The Franklin interrupts his own narrative in order to discuss marriage. Love, he says, should be based on freedom and mutual tolerance; any attempt to control the other person will drive love away. The most tolerant lover will be the most successful in the end, because things can be accomplished with patience that cannot be achieved by force. In any case, as everyone makes mistakes at some point, it is as well to learn tolerance before it is forced upon you. Thus, the knight promises his lady that he will be a patient husband and she promises him that she will be a faultless wife.

Marriage is one of the main themes of the tale and the Franklin interrupts his own narrative to make his views clear. This passage has been considered by many critics to offer a serious and successful account of a marriage based on freedom and equality. It sensibly points out the need for mutual tolerance, patience and lack of constraint; and yet, the world it presents is far from happy. In spite of the well-meaning Franklin's references to fluttering cupids and dear 'freendes', the most memorable line in the whole speech is the chilling 'Lerneth to suffre' (line 105); and his characters do not seem intent on taking the common-sense advice he offers. Everyone makes mistakes, the Franklin says, a split second before the lady promises 'ful wisly' (line 117) that her husband will never find any fault in her. (See Extended Commentaries, Text 1.)

89 **o** one

     saufly confidently

90 **freendes** lovers

     everich oother one another

     moot must

91 **holden compaignye** stay together

92 **maistrye** dominance

94 **Beteth** beats

95 **Love ... spirit free** love is a free spirit

96 **of kinde** by nature

97 **constreyned as a thral** forced like a slave

98 **sooth seyen shal** shall tell the truth

99 **pacient** long suffering

100 **He is ... above** he is in the highest position of all

102–3 **For it ... atteyne** for it wins out, as the clerks say, in situations where a severe approach would never succeed

104 **For every ... pleyne** there's no point arguing or complaining over every little word

105 **so moot I goon** I assure you

106 **wher so ye wole or noon** whether or not you want to

107 **wight** person

108 **That he ... amis** who does not do or say something wrong sometimes

109 **Ire** anger

     constellacioun influence of the planets

110 **Wyn** wine

     complexioun the body's constitutional balance. It was believed that the body was made up of four main elements known as 'humours' which determined both the health and temperament of the individual

112 **wreken** avenged

113–14 **After the time ... governaunce** anyone who is capable of self-control will restrain himself according to the occasion

116 **suffrance hire bihight** promised her he would be tolerant

118 **defaute in here** any fault in her

LINES 119–41   **The knight marries his lady but then goes to seek adventure in England**

The Franklin returns to his tale but soon digresses again. This time he considers the **paradox** that a man in love should be the woman's humble servant and, at the same time, her lord. The knight, whose name is Arveragus, marries his lady and they live together in great happiness. However, he then decides that, for the sake of his honour, he must leave his wife for a year or two and seek adventure in England.

> The Franklin's return to his tale does not sort out the matter of equality and mutual devotion in marriage. Instead, he becomes increasingly entangled in the concepts of servitude and lordship that are at the heart of both **courtly love** and medieval matrimony. The idea of the lady's devoted servant becoming her husband and lord is paradoxical, and the Franklin is not equipped to deal with the problem. He becomes repetitive and confused as he attempts to describe a relationship that goes beyond such terminology. However, the inadequacies here may not all be the Franklin's, for if he fails to give a convincing account of an ideal relationship, it may be because his society is so far removed from such equality and mutuality that it does not even possess the necessary vocabulary. Nevertheless, it remains a failure and as such does not bode well for Arveragus and his wife.

119 **wys accord** wise agreement

122 **servage** subjection

123 **in lordshipe above** in a state of supreme lordship

126 **The which ... acordeth to** with which the law of love agrees

129 **fer** far

Pedmark Penmark (in Finisterre)

130 **solas** comfort

131 **but he hadde wedded be** unless he has been married himself

136 **Kayrrud** Kerru

    cleped called

137 **Shoop hym** planned

    tweyne two

138 **eek** also

    Briteyne Britain

140 **For all … labour** for his heart was entirely set on this enterprise

LINES 142–74   Left behind, Dorigen grieves for her absent husband and is the cause of great concern to her friends

Dorigen is distraught at her husband's absence and weeps, complains, is unable to sleep and refuses to eat. Her anxious friends attempt to console her and eventually, like sculptors chipping away at a stone, they soothe her and her grief subsides. Letters from Arveragus also arrive saying that he will return to her soon and Dorigen is persuaded to be calm and to spend some time in the company of her friends.

> Our lady now has a name, Dorigen, but is still acting like a **stereotype**: one of the grief-stricken heroines of medieval literature, pining away for her knight. The narrator's observation that noble women behave like this 'whan hem liketh' (line 146) makes her complaint seem a little self-indulgent, and the piling on of verbs – 'She moorneth, waketh, waileth, fasteth, pleyneth' (line 147) – makes her seem excessive in her grief. Chaucer uses an interesting **simile** to describe her at this point, saying that her companions attempted to console her like sculptors chipping at a stone. Rock or stone is Dorigen's **symbol**, a sign of her stubborn, unyielding approach to the world. But yield she does in the end, joining her friends with a worryingly glib, 'For wel she saugh that it was for the beste' (line 174).

142 **stynten of** stop speaking of

144 **as hire hertes lyf** as much as her own life

145 **siketh** sighs

146 **As doon … liketh** as these noblewomen do when it pleases them

147 **She moorneth … pleyneth** she mourns, stays awake, laments, refuses to eat, complains

148 **hire so destreyneth** so afflicts her

149 **sette at noght** considered to be worth nothing

150 **hevy** gloomy

153 **causelees** without reason

sleeth hirself kills herself

155 **They doon ... bisinesse** they give her with all concern

157 **By proces** in due course

everichoon everyone

158 **graven in a stoon** chip away at a stone

159 **Til som figure ... be** until some image is imprinted upon it

162 **emprenting** imprint

163 **gan aswage** began to diminish

164 **duren** continue

swich rage such passionate grief

165 **care** sorrow

169 **slake** abate

171 **romen hire in compaignye** spend some time in their company

172 **derke fantasye** gloomy imaginings

LINES 175–222   **Dorigen becomes terror-stricken at the sight of the rocks in the sea and demands to know how a loving God could create such dangers**

Dorigen's castle stands on top of a cliff and from here she watches the ships sailing by, lamenting that none of them brings Arveragus back to her. She then turns her attention to the rocks at the foot of the cliff and the sight of them terrifies her so much that she collapses onto the grass. She cannot understand how God, who is good and all-powerful, can allow such fiendish rocks to exist. 'Do you not see, Lord, how they destroy mankind?' she demands. How can it be that God, who loves mankind and even created man in his own image, can also be the creator of something which seems to cause only death and destruction? Learned men, she muses, will no doubt tell her that everything is part of the divine plan, but for her part, she wishes that the rocks were cast down into hell.

The impatience that Dorigen had displayed at Arveragus's absence reaches crisis point as she questions God himself. With typical exaggeration, she laments the 'hundred thousand bodies' (line 205) slain by the rocks. It seems to her as though the world is chaotic and frightening and there is no evidence of any divine plan (lines 197–9). But *seems* is the operative word here. This passage is full of references to 'seeming' and 'seeing', and, as always in this tale, perception is found to be false. Dorigen's problem is that she *cannot* see. The scholars she dismisses would have been able to explain it to her: man's view of the world is partial and thus full of illusions. There is a plan but the mind of man is not capable of grasping it in its entirety. Just as someone standing in London cannot really 'see' London, Dorigen sitting staring at the rocks cannot comprehend the whole plan. It is not, in fact, the world that is out of control, it is Dorigen herself.

175 **faste** close
177 **Hire to disporte … heigh** to amuse herself high up upon the cliff top
178 **seigh** saw
179 **where as hem liste go** going wherever they pleased
180 **parcel** part
183 **were** would be
184 **warisshed** cured
peynes smerte pain of sorrow
189 **That on hire feet … sustene** that she was not able to remain standing
192 **sikes colde** gloomy sighs
193 **Eterne** eternal
purveiaunce providence
199 **Ledest** govern
certein governaunce sure control
195 **In idel** without purpose
seyn say
196 **grisly** horrible
feendly fiendish
197–9 **That semen … stable** that seem more like a foul confused piece of work than the fair creation of such a perfect, wise and unchanging God
200 **wroght** created
202 **nis yfostred man** no man benefits
204 **how mankynde it destroyeth** it destroys mankind

206–8 **Han rokkes ... merk** have been slain on the rocks, although they are forgotten, while mankind is so important a part of your creation that you made him in your own image

209 **chiertee** love

211 **That ye swiche ... destroyen** that you provide the means to destroy them

212 **anoyen** cause trouble

213 **I woot wel ... leste** I know well that scholars will say as they please

215 **Though I ... yknowe** although I am not able to understand the reasons

216 **thilke** that same

217 **As kepe my lord** may he keep my lord safe

218 **lete I al disputison** I leave all disputation

219 **wolde God** I wish to God

221 **Thise rokkes ... feere** fear of these rocks is killing my heart

LINES 223–52   **The group of friends takes Dorigen to a beautiful garden**

Dorigen's friends realise that walks by the seashore are doing more harm than good and take her elsewhere, attempting to distract her with dancing and games. It is now 6 May, and they arrange to spend the day in a garden so beautiful that it rivals paradise itself, its fresh loveliness bringing joy to all but the most sorrowful heart. There is singing and dancing after dinner but Dorigen remains alone, finding no pleasure in such games without Arveragus. Still, she feels hope once more and her grief has subsided.

> May gardens are frequently the landscape of love in medieval literature and this one is to be no exception. However, it is a slightly worrying place. It is described as 'verray paradis' (line 240) but it is highly artificial too. The garden is certainly beautiful but those inside it may be just a bit too light-hearted (line 242), too concerned with games (line 228) and inclined to 'pleyen' a little too much (lines 225 and 228). (See Extended Commentaries, Text 2.)

223 **disport** pleasure

224 **disconfort** distressing

225 **shopen** arranged

227 **delitables** delightful

228 **tables** backgammon

229 **morwe-tide** morning

231 **maad hir ordinaunce** made arrangements

232 **Of vitaille** regarding food

purveiaunce provisions

234 **sixte** sixth

235 **Which May ... shoures** and May with its gentle showers had painted

237 **craft of mannes hand** the skilful hands of men

curiously elaborately

239 **prys** excellence

240 **But if** unless

the verray paradis paradise itself

244 **to greet** very great

248 **moone** lament

251 **a time abide** wait for a time

252 **slide** slip away

LINES 253–87   **A squire named Aurelius is secretly in love with Dorigen**

Amongst the dancers is a young squire named Aurelius, a lively, talented, virtuous and wise young man, and one of the most handsome ever to have lived. Aurelius has been secretly in love with Dorigen for more than two years but has only dared to speak of it in the songs he composes. He is tormented by his love, driven almost to the point of despair, and reduced to gazing longingly upon his lady's face at public gatherings. Dorigen, however, remains entirely unaware of his feelings.

The description of Aurelius is everything that we would expect of a medieval **courtly lover**: he is handsome, accomplished and noble, and keeps the rules of love as he secretly pines for Dorigen. Like the other characters, he is first presented as a **stereotype**, though as always there are some individualising touches. He is notably compared to a Fury in hell (line 278), a **simile** which links him with Dorigen and her 'hellish rocks', for both he and Dorigen manage to create a hell out of their situations. And like Dorigen too, Aurelius does everything to excess: why write a song for his lady, if he can compose, 'manye layes, / Songes, compleintes, roundels, virelayes' (lines 275–6), all of which are very voluble ways of expressing his inability to express his love.

254 **squier** young knight

biforn in front of

255 **fressher** more lively

jolier of array more gaily dressed

256 **As to my doom** in my opinion

257 **passinge** better than

258 **sith that** since

259 **discrive** describe

260 **Oon of … on live** one of the most handsome men alive

261 **wys** wise

262 **holden in greet prys** held in high esteem

263 **sothe** truth

264 **Unwiting … at al** entirely without Dorigen's knowledge

265 **lusty** pleasant

268 **aventure** fortune

269 **dorste** dared

270 **Withouten coppe … penaunce** he suffered without measure

271 **despeyred** in despair

272 **wreye** reveal

273 **as in a general compleyning** as if it were part of a general lament

274 **no thing** not at all

275 **layes** songs

276 **roundels** rondeaux

virelayes virelays. Both rondeaux and virelays were songs with refrains intended to be sung to a dance in a 'ronde' or circle

278 **furye** in classical mythology, the three Furies tormented souls in the Underworld. They were sometimes described as howling creatures tearing at their own flesh

279–80 **Ekko … Narcisus** the nymph Echo fell in love with the beautiful Narcissus but, when he did not return her love, she wasted away until nothing was left but her voice

281–2 **In oother … biwreye** he did not dare reveal his sorrow in any other way than I have told you here

283 **paraventure** perhaps

284 **kepen hir observaunces** have their social events

286 **In swich ... grace** like a man who asks for mercy

287 **wiste** knew

   entente intent

LINES 288–306   Aurelius tells Dorigen of his love

Dorigen has known Aurelius for a long time, as a neighbour and a man of good reputation, and the two of them fall into conversation. Aurelius, however, sees his opportunity and tells Dorigen that he is in love with her, declaring that he would have gladly gone over the sea himself and never come back if he thought it would make her happy. He knows, he says, that his love is in vain and that the breaking of his heart will be the only reward for his loyal service, and yet, one word from her could save him. He begs only for her mercy.

> There is something insidious about the way in which 'moore and moore, / Unto his purpos drough Aurelius' (lines 292–3) until he sees his opportunity. It is a dramatic declaration, full of the language of **courtly love** (*servyce, gerdon, reweth*); and it is also manifestly untrue. Aurelius does not wish that he had gone over the sea with Arveragus; what he really wishes is that Dorigen will take pity upon him and agree to become his lover. The image he presents of the loyal servant of love, willing to die if it will make his lady happy, is thus just another illusion in a tale which has already called into question the nature of truth and reality.

288 **er they thennes went** before they left that place

290 **worshipe** good reputation

291 **And hadde ... yoore** and she had known him for a long time

293 **drough** drew

296 **So that ... glade** if I knew that it would make your heart glad

297 **wolde** wish

300 **woot** know

301 **gerdon** reward

   but only

302 **reweth** take pity

   peynes smerte agonising suffering

303 **sleen** kill

304 **grave** buried

305 **leiser** time

    seye speak

306 **do me deye** cause my death

Lines 307–39   **Dorigen rejects Aurelius but then adds that she would grant his request if he could remove all the rocks from the sea**

Dorigen firmly states that she will never be unfaithful to her husband, swearing before God that this is her final answer. However, she then adds 'in pley' that she would indeed love Aurelius if he were able to remove all the treacherous rocks from the coast of Brittany so that the ships could come safely to harbour. This, she knows, is an impossibility and so she dismisses Aurelius, demanding to know what business he has loving another man's wife. Aurelius too regards the task as impossible and declares that he must now die of his unrequited love.

> This passage has caused a great deal of debate amongst critics who cannot decide whether Dorigen is being cruel, too lenient, or has a subconscious desire to be unfaithful to her husband. Her immediate response is unequivocal as Chaucer heaps negatives into her speech to make her answer a very firm 'no'. The problem is what happens next as Dorigen adds 'in pley' (line 316) the silly business about the rocks. However, she then states very clearly that she knows no-one could ever perform the task she has set and follows this up with a very blunt account of a husband's sexual rights, intended to cool the ardour of any suitor. Her response is, therefore, three-quarters flat rejection and one part 'pley'. It is not clear why she does this: she seems too firm to be really teasing Aurelius, who has no hope left after she has finished speaking; love for her husband no doubt plays its part, the threatening rocks still being at the forefront of her mind. However, the clue to the real reason may be in the word 'pley'. It has already featured strongly in the tale as the young nobles gathered in the garden, for 'pley' is what is expected of noblemen and especially noblewomen. Dorigen is used to playing the role of

courtly lady: that's how the tale began and now, less than 300 lines later, she finds herself in that role again. Faced with the extremely courtly Aurelius, she thinks she can rise to the challenge, act the courtly mistress, soften the blow and defuse the situation. She is wrong.

309 **erst** before

311 **thilke** that same

yaf gave

313 **ne werk** nor deed

as fer as I have wit to the best of my knowledge

314 **knit** bound by marriage

319 **Sin I ... complaine** since I see that you lament so pitifully

320 **Looke what day** whatever day

endelong all along [the coast] of

321 **stoon** stone

322 **That they ... goon** so that they do not hinder any ship or boat

324 **ysene** to be seen

326 **trouthe** promise

in al that evere I kan to the best of my ability

327 **grace** mercy

329 **bitide** happen

331-2 **What deyntee ... wyf** what pleasure can it be for a man to go loving another man's wife

333 **whan so** whenever

him liketh it pleases him

334 **siketh** sighs

337 **inpossible** impossibility

338 **Thanne moot ... horrible** so I must die a sudden and horrible death

LINES 340–72 Aurelius prays to Apollo, god of the sun, for help

They are interrupted by the rest of the group who roam happily through the garden, unaware of what has gone on between Dorigen and Aurelius. The setting sun is a signal to all of them to return home and they move off joyfully, all except Aurelius who goes home in a state of anguish, feeling that he must die of love. In a frenzy he appeals to Apollo, the god of the sun, who brings life to all things in harmony with on the time and season. Only Apollo's merciful intervention, he feels, can save him and he proceeds to explain how this can be achieved.

> Aurelius, who has been complaining to Dorigen ever since he opened his mouth in this tale, now directs his lament to a higher power. His misery is intense, and the language of the passage indicates that his love has brought him to the brink of insanity as 'raving ... out of his wit ... He niste what he spak' (lines 354–6). His loss of control is similar to what Dorigen had earlier felt, and, like her, he too addresses a higher power. But while Dorigen had been seeking reassurance that there was benevolent order in the universe, Aurelius is seeking to break down that order. Apollo is described as the 'governour' (line 359) of nature, allotting a time and season to every flower and plant. Losing control, Aurelius wants nature itself to lose control so that he can fulfil his unnatural desire for Dorigen.

341 **aleyes** garden paths

romeden wandered

344 **hewe** brightness

345 **For th'orisonte ... light** for the horizon has robbed the sun of his light

347 **solas** delight

350 **asterte** escape

353 **knowes** knees

354 **orisoun** prayer

355 **For verray wo ... breyde** he was out of his mind with grief

356 **niste** did not know

357 **pleynt** lament

358 **goddes** gods

sonne sun

359 **Appollo** Apollo, god of the sun, which gives everything life

361 **yevest** gives

after thy declinacion according to your position

363 **herberwe** astrological house

364 **Phebus** Phoebus, another name for Apollo, meaning 'bright'

eighe eye

365 **but lorn** utterly lost

366 **hath my deeth ysworn** has decreed my death

367–8 **Withoute gilt … pitee** without any fault of mine, unless you, in your mercy, have some pity on my dying heart

369 **lest** please

371 **Now voucheth … devise** now allow me to describe to you

372 **holpen** helped

wise way

LINES 373–414   Aurelius asks for the help of Diana, goddess of the moon

Working on the principle that the tides are controlled by the waxing and waning of the moon, Aurelius wants Apollo to appeal to his sister Diana, goddess of the moon, to make the tides permanently high. In this way, the rocks will disappear under fathoms of water and he will be able to claim Dorigen. Alternatively, Diana could use her powers as goddess of the underworld to remove the rocks to the depths of hell where they can do no harm. Aurelius tearfully begs for the god's help, promising to go on a barefoot pilgrimage to his temple, and finally collapses in a faint.

> Aurelius's plan is dependent upon Diana, but it is interesting that he does not appeal to her directly, praying instead to her brother to bring about his desires. The fact is that women are not permitted to have power in this tale, not even goddesses. Diana, goddess of chastity, is a weak figure here, featuring in a plan to force a woman into adultery. As queen of the underworld Diana is called Proserpina, famously raped by Pluto, its king (lines 402–3); and as Lucina, the goddess is depicted as craving her brother's light, following him 'ful bisily' (line 379). Dorigen's fate will, in the end, be decided by men as they come to an arrangement with one another, and a similar male bargain is being made here. But the plans are, in fact, nonsense. Even if the moon did perform the miracle of circling the earth at the same rate as the sun, the tide would not remain high. Aurelius is simply mistaken. As for his second plan, casting the rocks into hell, this is exactly what Dorigen had had in mind (lines 219–20). Both squire and lady have wept, wailed, spoken to their gods, been entirely irrational, and settled in the end on the same useless prayer.

373 **Lucina the sheene** the bright Lucina. Lucina is one of the names of Diana, goddess of the moon

375 **Neptunus** Neptune. Neptune is the ancient god of the sea, but the sea's movements are controlled by the moon and thus, ultimately, by Lucina

378 **quiked** kindled

     fir fire

382 **moore and lesse** great and small

385 **opposicion** opposition of sun and moon i.e. time of high tide

386 **Leon** Leo

387 **As preieth hire** to ask her

388 **fadme** fathoms

     overspringe rise above

390 **endure** last

392 **Holdeth youre heste** keep your promise

394 **Preye** ask

     go no faster cours go at the same speed

397-8 **Thanne shal …day** then she will always be in opposition to you and the spring flood-tides will last night and day

399-400 **And but … deere** but if she will not consent to give me my supreme, dear lady in this way

403 **Pluto** god of the underworld. Diana, here, is queen of the underworld as well as goddess of the moon

405 **Delphos** Delphi in Greece, a main centre for the worship of Apollo

408 **in swowne** in a faint

410 **penaunce** suffering

412 **Dispeyred** in despair

413-14 **Lete I … die** I leave this sorrowful creature lying there; as far as I'm concerned he can make up his own mind whether he will live or die

Lines 415–28   Arveragus returns home

Arveragus returns home as a hero, the very flower of chivalry, and Dorigen is overjoyed to have her husband back. He greets her without suspicion, not doubting her fidelity for a moment, and the two of them live blissfully together, dancing, attending jousts, and enjoying each other's company.

The Franklin leaves Aurelius in mortal torment and turns his attention to Arveragus, newly returned from England. The contrast between the two men is great: our handsome squire has become the 'sike Aurelius' (line 428), while Arveragus is triumphant and 'with heele (prosperity)' (line 415). The description of the knight is wholly positive and, at this point at least, he is without the fantasies and illusions that torment the other characters. The vocabulary of honourable knighthood and 'joye and blisse' (line 427) come together in this passage in a way that suggests that a good chivalric life is how happiness is achieved.

415 **heele** prosperity

419 **lusty** valiant

420 **fresshe** bold

422 **No thing list ... imaginatif** it did not occur to him to be suspicious

423 **wight** man

425 **noght entendeth to** he pays no attention to

426 **justeth** jousts
   maketh hire good cheere entertains her

LINES 429–43   Aurelius continues to suffer

Aurelius lives in torment for more than two years, unable to face the world and confiding only in his brother. His love is like an arrow that has pierced his heart. Worse, it is like a *sursanure*, a wound that has healed on the surface but still festers underneath, making a cure almost impossible.

With the image of the happy active life of Arveragus still in our heads we return to the languishing love-sickness of Aurelius. He is still behaving like an archetypal **courtly lover**, prostrate with grief but keeping his sorrow secret from everyone except one trusted male confidant, just as the books describe. To prove his courtly credentials he is even compared to one of literature's love-lorn heroes, though the Franklin could perhaps have thought of someone more inspiring than Pamphilus (line 438). The 'love as sickness' **metaphor** has developed to become the most dangerous kind of wound (lines 439–43).

429 **langour** suffering
    furius raging
431 **Er any foot ... gon** before he could set foot in the world again
434 **werk** trouble
436 **dorste** dared
    seyn speak
437 **Under his ... secree** he bore it more secretly in his heart
438 **Pamphilus for Galathee** Pamphilus was the hero of a medieval Latin poem, wounded by his love for Galatea
439 **his brest ... sene** his breast looked from the outside to be unwounded
440 **arwe kene** piercing arrow
441 **sursanure** wound healed only on the surface

LINES 444–92   **The brother of Aurelius has an idea: they could use natural magic to make the rocks disappear**

Aurelius's brother attempts to help him and remembers a book of natural magic that he had seen once while studying in Orleans. Such magic, interrupts the Franklin, is, of course, mere nonsense, but the brother is excited by his idea and remembers the conjurers he has seen at court who could make a boat sail through the hall, or a lion or field of flowers appear. It occurs to him that such a magician could make it look as though Dorigen's rocks had vanished. Thus, Aurelius could make her keep her promise, or at least have the pleasure of shaming her if she refused to keep her word.

> Dorigen's original request had been that the dangerous rocks should be removed from the sea 'stoon by stoon' (line 321). In spite of this, Aurelius's prayer to the gods was only for a high tide to make it seem that the rocks had gone. Now his brother has similar plans for illusion, suggesting that they use natural magic to deal with the problem. While natural magic was regarded in the Middle Ages as a legitimate science, it is clear that there is something underhand about the plan. The brother weeps 'prively', remembers a book left 'prively' on a desk, and says 'prively' to himself that all shall be well. He does not seem to imagine for a moment that the rocks could be removed, merely that some court conjuring trick could be used to make it seem to 'mannes sighte' (line 479) that they were gone.

Then 'moste she nedes holden hire biheste' (line 491) he says. He thinks of Dorigen merely as 'she', the nameless object of his brother's lust. Worse, if she does not yield, they can at least publicly humiliate her. This is not the language of true love: it is a petty, vengeful desire to inflict pain on a woman he does not even dignify with a name.

444 **prively** secretly

446 **Orliens** Orleans

447 **been lykerous** are eager

448 **To reden ... curious** to study the occult arts

449 **Seken in ... herne** look in every nook and cranny

452 **At Orliens ... say** while studying at Orleans he had seen a book

453 **magik natureel** natural magic

felawe friend

455 **Al were he ther** even though he was there

456 **Hadde prively ... ylaft** which he had left covered up upon his desk

458 **Touchinge** concerning

mansiouns astrological houses

459 **longen to** pertain to

swich folye other such nonsense

461–2 **For hooly ... greve** for the faith of Holy Church in our creed does not allow us to be harmed by illusion

466 **warisshed hastily** soon cured

467 **siker** certain

468 **apparences** illusions

469 **Swiche as ... pleye** like those performed by all those clever magicians

473 **rowen** row

474 **grim leoun** fierce lion

475 **mede** meadow

477 **lym and stoon** bricks and mortar

478 **And whan ... anon** and when it pleased them, made it disappear at once

483 **above** in addition

487 **weren yvoided** had disappeared

everichon every one

488 **brinke** cliffs

comen and gon come and go

489 **And in swich ... two** and stay like that for a week or two

491 **Thanne moste ... biheste** then she must keep her promise

492 **atte leeste** at least

LINES 493–516   The two brothers encounter a magician

Aurelius jumps up immediately when he hears his brother's plan and the two of them leave at once for Orleans. Not far from the city they encounter one of its scholars who politely greets them in Latin and miraculously tells them that he knows their reason for coming and what they want there. They ask this clerk about former friends and fellow students but are told that they are all dead. The clerk then takes them to his home, the best-stocked and most comfortable house Aurelius has ever seen.

> The clerk flourishes his learned Latin almost like a business card, a sign of his credentials, for in essence he is a businessman, and his well-stocked house is a sign of his success. The fact that all the brother's former companions are now dead casts a sombre air over this encounter (lines 507–9). This is no wand-waving magician of fairy tale about to perform magic that will make everyone live happily ever after. He operates in a world in which people die and others 'weep ful ofte many a teere' (line 510).

495 **yaf** gave

496 **up stirte anon** leapt up at once

497 **forthward** forwards

is he fare he is gone

498 **lissed** relieved

500 **But if it ... thre** only two or three furlongs from it

502 **thriftily hem grette** greeted them politely

506 **al that was in hire entente** their whole purpose for coming

507 **felawes** friends

508 **olde dawes** the old days

509 **dede** dead

511 **lighte** dismounted

513 **maden hem wel at ese** made themselves comfortable

514 **vitaille** food

515–16 **So wel ... noon** Aurelius had never in his life seen such a well-run house as that one

LINES 517–36   The clerk causes great wonders to appear

The clerk conjures up forests and great numbers of wild deer that are then killed by hounds or else wounded by huntsmen. Other hunters fly hawks by the river and kill the heron, while knights can be seen jousting nearby. Then, to the great delight of Aurelius, he sees Dorigen at a dance and he himself is dancing with her. But, at a clap of the magician's hands, all these wondrous sights disappear and the three men are alone again in the clerk's study.

> Everything the clerk causes to appear is designed to appeal to a courtly young man like Aurelius. There is hunting, hawking and jousting, the standard pastimes of medieval noblemen, but these are not altogether pretty visions. The harts are 'slain with houndes' (line 521), the heron are with 'haukes ... slain' (line 525), and the jousting knights are putting their lives in danger. The culmination of these horrible pleasures is the vision of Aurelius dancing with Dorigen. Death and destruction are everywhere and Aurelius's passion is no less destructive. The traditional image of Cupid shooting his darts in a garden of love has been replaced by a forest full of deer bleeding to death from arrow wounds (line 522). There is nothing positive about this love; it is not even real. The clerk claps his hands and 'al oure revel was ago' (line 532). Like so much in this tale, it was merely illusory.

517 **er** before
sopeer supper
519 **hertes** harts
hornes hye great antlers
520 **ye** eye
522 **arwes** arrows
blede bleed
523 **voided** vanished
524 **fauconers** hunters with falcons
river hawking ground

525 **That with hir ... slain** who slew the heron with their hawks

526 **justing** jousting

527 **he dide him swich plesaunce** he delighted him very much

530 **maister** master

wroughte created

531 **Saugh** saw

clapte clapped

532 **revel** revelry

ago gone

533 **remoeved they nevere** they never went

536 **no wight** no-one

LINES 537–66   The men negotiate a price for the clerk's help

After supper, the men discuss the removal of the rocks from the coast of Brittany and the clerk says that he will not perform the task for less than 1,000 pounds of gold. Aurelius readily agrees to the amount, declaring that he would give the whole world if it were his. He and the clerk exchange solemn promises and Aurelius retires to bed, happy at the prospect of the bargain he has made.

> The language of knightly honour and **courtly love** is still present in this passage but it no longer refers to the passion of a lover or the loyalty of a vassal. 'Gerdon' (line 548), the 'reward' which the courtly lover begs from his lady for his loyal service as Aurelius did earlier (line 301), has become merely the amount involved in a business transaction; 'trouthe' (line 559), the code of honour by which a knight lives, is nothing more than a sworn deal; and 'feith' (line 562), the mainstay of medieval life, has become merely a contractual term. The great medieval lover, traditionally so tormented that he is unable to eat or sleep, enjoys a hearty supper and 'al that night he hadde his reste' (line 564).

539 **undertake** declare

540 **Sith I yow bad** since I asked you

543 **whan it liketh yow** whenever you like

544 **though ye wol right now** even if you want it immediately

545–6 **Go we ... reste** 'It is best that we go dine,' he said. 'Even people in love must rest sometime'

547 **fille they in tretee**   they began negotiating

548 **somme**   amount

     gerdon   payment

550 **from Gerounde to the mouth of Saine**   from the river Gironde to the mouth of the river Seine

551 **made it straunge**   raised difficulties

557 **yeve**   give

558 **ful drive**   completed

     knit   agreed

559 **by my trouthe**   upon my word of honour

560–1 **But looketh ... to-morwe**   but take care now that neither negligence nor laziness on your part keeps us here any later than tomorrow

562 **have heer my feith to borwe**   I give you my word

563 **whan him leste**   when it pleased him

565 **What for**   on account of

566 **His woful ... lisse**   his sorrowful heart had relief from its suffering

LINES 567–83   It is near Christmas when Aurelius returns to Brittany with the clerk

The group sets off the next day and returns to Brittany. It is now December and the sun, having entered the astrological house of Capricorn, is low in the sky and a pale, metallic colour. The days of bright, golden sunshine are long gone and instead frost, sleet and rain have ravaged every garden. It is the time of the god Janus, looking back to the old year and forward to the new, warming himself before a roaring fire and feasting on boar's flesh, while the whole world cries 'Merry Christmas'.

It is unusual to find the passing of the seasons mentioned in a medieval **romance** but *The Franklin's Tale* makes several references to the month and the weather. Aurelius first approached Dorigen in a Maytime garden and now it is midwinter, a time of hardship and apparent death as the frost, sleet and rain, 'Destroyed hath the grene in every yerd' (line 579). However, death here is only an illusion, for the seeds of renewal are present at all times as spring inevitably follows winter. There is order and hope in the universe and the presence of the god Janus assures us of this. He is not just a winter deity: he looks backwards but also forwards, and is positioned here in the middle of the tale. The tale and the year have reached their darkest points, as the sun shines 'ful pale' (line 577) and Aurelius employs his magician, but the year is now beginning its own process of renewal and with it comes the hope that all shall be well.

568 **righte way** direct route

570 **been descended** got down

     ther where

573–5 **Phebus ... brighte** the sun, which had shone in the summer like burnished gold, with bright beams, was reaching the end of the solar year and had a pale metallic sheen

576 **Capricorn** the sun enters the astrological house of Capricorn in December and is at its lowest point in the sky during this time

578 **reyn** rain

579 **yerd** garden

580 **Janus ... berd** Janus, with his two bearded faces, sat by the fire. Janus was the Roman god of doorways, beginnings and endings, and was usually depicted with two faces looking in opposite directions. The month of January is derived from his name as he was associated with the threshold of the year, looking back to the old and forward to the new

581 **bugle horn** drinking-horn (made from the horn of the 'bugle' or wild ox)

582–3 **Biforn ... man** the flesh of a roasted boar is placed before him, and every happy man cries 'Merry Christmas!'

LINES 584–624   The clerk makes the rocks disappear

Aurelius attends the clerk, begging him either to remove the rocks or pierce his heart with a sword so that he can end his suffering. The clerk pities him and works night and day to perform the task, making many complicated astrological calculations – a process which is described at length by the Franklin – until the time is right and it seems as though the rocks have disappeared.

Chaucer himself was an expert in astrology, but this passage need not be taken too seriously. The clerk's actions are intended to sound impressive but are meant to remain mysterious. The most important point is the repeated reference to 'seeming': 'illusioun' (line 592), 'apparence or jogelrye' (line 593), and the final declaration that 'It *semed* that alle the rokkes were aweye' (line 624). The rocks are not gone, it is merely the grandest illusion in a tale filled with them.

584–5 **Aurelius ... reverence** Aurelius entertains and deals respectfully with this expert in magic to the best of his ability

586 **doon his diligence** do his best

588 **Or with ... herte** or else he begs that the magician will slit open his heart with a sword

589 **subtil** learned

routhe pity

590–1 **That night ... conclusioun** that night and day he was on the watch for a chance to perform his experiment

593 **jogelrye** conjuror's trick

594 **I ne kan no** I do not know any

595 **That she ... seye** so that she and everyone else should believe and say

599 **japes** tricks

wrecchednesse wretched work

600 **supersticious cursednesse** diabolic wickedness

601 **tables Tolletanes** astronomical tables

602 **ne ther lakked nought** there was nothing lacking there

603 **Neither ... yeeris** neither his tables for the motion of planets in twenty-year cycles nor those for planetary position in any given year

604 **rootes** dates

geeris apparatus

605 **As been ... argumentz** such as his table of distances and his angles for calculations

606 **proporcioneles convenientz** tables for computing planetary motions

608 **eighte speere** the eighth sphere. The sphere enclosing the universe in which the stars are set

609–11 **He knew ... considered is** he knew how far the star Alnath had moved away from the fixed point of the house of Aries above, which can be observed from the ninth sphere

612 **kalkuled** calculated

613 **mansioun** position of the moon

614 **He knew ... proporcioun** he could calculate all the other positions with his astrological tables

616 **face, and terme** each house of the zodiac was divided into equal parts known as *faces* and unequal parts known as *termes*

618 **Acordaunt to** in accordance with

620 **meschaunces** evil practices

621 **useden** performed

    thilke dayes those days

623 **wyke or tweye** week or two

LINES 625–66   Aurelius reminds Dorigen of her promise

Aurelius falls at the feet of the magician in gratitude and then goes to the temple where he knows he will find Dorigen. He approaches her in humility and fear, saying that he would not wish to displease her for the world, but ... the rocks are gone!

> The above synopsis may seem very brief for forty-two lines of text, but it takes Aurelius a very long time to get to the point. He still maintains the pose of **courtly lover** but he is a courtly lover with a definite agenda. He still begs for her love as a loyal servant but words such as 'biheste' (line 663) and 'trouthe' (line 656) are creeping into his vocabulary. The servant of love who, according to tradition, is not worthy of his lady's love, has become wheedlingly insistent and legalistic. The courtly veneer is wearing thin. (See Extended Commentaries, Text 3.)

625 **which that yet despeired is** who is still in a state of despair

626 **Wher** whether

    han have

    amis badly

629 **voided** removed

630 **fil** fell

636 **anon-right** immediately

637 **dredful** fearful

    cheere expression

638 **Salewed hath** has greeted

639 **righte** own true

640 **drede** fear

641 **And lothest ... displese** and would be most loathe to displease of all the people in the world

642 **Nere it** were it not

 disese distress

643 **dien** die

645 **outher** either

 pleyne tell my sorrow

646 **Ye sle ... peyne** guiltless, I am dying of the sorrow you cause me

647 **routhe** pity

648 **Aviseth ... trouthe** consider this before you break your promise

651 **woot** know

 hight promised

652–3 **Nat that ... grace** not that I am claiming anything from you, my supreme lady, as a legal right, I ask only for your mercy

655 **bihighten** promised

656 **youre trouthe plighten ye** you gave me your word

662 **vouche sauf** agree to it

663 **Dooth as yow list** do as you please

 biheste promise

664 **quik** alive

665 **In yow ... deye** you have the power to make me live or die

LINES 667–94 **Dorigen thinks that death would be preferable to keeping her promise to Aurelius**

Dorigen stands in a state of shock, the blood drained from her face. 'Alas,' she says, 'I never imagined that such an unnatural thing could happen'. She goes home, weeping, wailing and fainting but tells no-one about her encounter with Aurelius. She laments her fate, seeing no way forward except death or dishonour: either she must keep her promise to Aurelius and dishonour herself in adultery; or she must refuse to keep her promise and dishonour herself by breaking her word. Faced with these options, she feels that her own death would be preferable. After all, she muses, she has history on her side, for haven't there been many wives and maidens who chose death over the violation of their bodies?

 The only thing worse than having a prayer go unanswered, Dorigen realises, is having it answered. Her weeping and wailing is familiar from earlier in the tale but this is even more intense. For the second time she makes a 'compleynt' (line 682) but this one is more accurately addressed to Fortune. She may still be uncontrollably grief-stricken but she has at least learned to direct her complaints towards a more worthy recipient. She remains, however, her over-dramatic self and so quickly moves on to thoughts of suicide. The role of courtly lady is being swapped for that of tragic heroine.

669 **She wende ... trappe** she never expected to fall into such a trap

671 **by possibilitee** by any possibility

672 **monstre** unnatural thing

merveille marvel

675 **For verray ... go** her terrible fear meant that she could scarcely walk

677 **swowneth** fainted

678 **But why ... shee** but she did not tell anyone why

681 **cheere** countenance

682 **compleynt** lament

683 **on thee, Fortune, I pleyne** I am complaining against you, Fortune. Fortune was frequently depicted as a blind goddess, turning humanity on a large wheel, which raised them up to success and riches or down to poverty and ruin. Dorigen imagines herself chained to this wheel

684 **unwar** unexpectedly

cheyne chain

685 **Fro which ... socour** I know of nothing which can help me escape

687 **Oon of ... chese** I must choose one of these two

688-9 **have I levere to lese / My lyf** I would rather die

690 **lese my name** lose my good name

691 **And with ... ywis** and, indeed, my death can cancel out the debt

693 **yslain** killed

694 **Rather ... trespas** rather than commit a sin with her body

LINES 695–784 **Dorigen lists the famous women in history who died rather than be dishonoured**

As she contemplates suicide, Dorigen calls to mind all the women of history and legend who preferred to die rather than face dishonour. She recalls first of all the stories of virgins who died rather than be raped: women such as the daughters of King Phidon who fled from their father's slayers and drowned themselves in a well, or Stymphalis who was murdered as she clung to the statue of the goddess of chastity. Dorigen then turns her mind to wives who acted in a similar way, such as Hasdrubal's wife who burned to death with her children rather than surrender to the Romans, or Lucretia who committed suicide after she had been raped in order to spare her family the shame. It seems to Dorigen that she must share the fate of these women and she lists many more examples to prove her point.

> Ancient and medieval history often worked on the principle that the only good woman was a dead one, and was particularly fond of those women who were considerate enough to take their own lives. Dorigen has, therefore, a lengthy list of virtuous examples to emulate, and names almost all of them in her forty-eight-hour marathon complaint. She begins with the much honoured virgins of history who died in order to preserve their chastity. Then she moves on to the wives who acted in a similar way. By the time she gets to the concubine of Alcebiades (lines 767–9), however, her examples are not strictly relevant. This woman was not being sexually threatened, she gave up her life in order to see that her lover's body was buried. Similarly, the story of the wife of Alcestis who loved her husband so much that she died in his place (line 770), may be moving but it has little to do with Dorigen's situation. Teuta, honoured here for her 'wyfly chastitee' (line 781), was not even married, and Bilia's claim to fame was putting up with her husband's bad breath (line 783). The list begins in all seriousness, considering the fates of women for whom 'honour' could only mean sexual honour, but Dorigen cannot sustain such an account and her complaint collapses into a list of mausoleum-building, nurse-murdering, halitosis-tolerating women. Emotion has once more overcome Dorigen and her great speech on the fate of women becomes increasingly irrational and absurd.

696 **thritty tirauntz** thirty tyrants
   cursednesse wickedness
697 **Phidon** the Thirty Tyrants seized power in Athens in the fifth century BC. Legend has it that they killed King Phidon and ordered his virgin daughters to be stripped naked and brought before them to dance on the floor stained

with their father's blood. The women escaped and committed suicide by jumping into a well

698 **for t'areste** to be arrested

699 **in d espit** by force

702 **God yeve hem meschaunce** curses upon them

704 **lese** lose

maidenhede virginity

705 **prively** secretly

been stirt leapt

706 **dreynte hemselven** drowned themselves

707–9 **They of ... lecherye** the men of Messene had enquiries and searches made for fifty Spartan virgins upon whom they could vent their lechery

711 **nas** was not

711–13 **with a good ... maidenhede** and willingly chose to die rather than to lose her virginity through rape

716 **heet Stymphalides** who was called Stymphalis. Stymphalis fled from the tyrant Aristoclides who had killed her father and wanted to rape her. She sought refuge in the temple of Diana, goddess of chastity, and clung to the goddess's statue until she was stabbed to death

719 **hente** grasped

image statue

721 **No wight ... arace** no-one could prise her hands from it

722 **selve** same

723 **sith** since

despit aversion

724 **To been defouled...delit** to be defiled by men taking their foul pleasure

727 **Hasdrubales wyf** Hasdrubal was king of Carthage in 146 BC when it was burnt to the ground by the Romans. Rather than surrender, his wife snatched up her children and leapt into the flames

732 **Than any Romayn ... vileynye** than that any Roman should dishonour her

733 **Lucresse** Lucretia was raped by Tarquinius Sextus and killed herself rather than bring dishonour to her husband

736 **name** good name

737 **Milesie** Miletus was sacked by the Gauls in 276 BC. There are several ancient accounts of the seven virgins who chose death rather than surrender to the invading army

741 **as touchinge this mateere** relating to this matter

742 **Habradate** when King Abradates was killed, his wife Panthea committed suicide

745–6 **And seyde ... may** and said, 'At least no man shall defile my body, if I have anything to do with it'

747 **mo** more

754 **Demociones doghter** after the death of the man she was due to marry, Demotion's virgin daughter felt that any future betrothal would be tantamount to bigamy and killed herself

756 **Cedasus** the daughters of Scedasus killed one another after they were raped

758 **for swich a manere cas** in a similar situation

760 **Nichanore** when the city of Thebes was captured in 336 BC an officer named Nicanor desired a virgin captive who consequently killed herself

763 **Macidonye** ancient legend tells of a virgin from Thebes who killed her Macedonian rapist and then herself

764 **She with ... redressed** she avenged her lost virginity with her death

765 **Nicerates wyf** after her husband was put to death by the Thirty Tyrants of Athens, the wife of Niceratus killed herself

766 **That for swich cas ... lyf** who killed herself in a similar situation

767–9 **How trewe ... be** also, how loyal the lover of Alcibiades was, who chose to die rather than allow his body to be left unburied. Timandra, the mistress of the murdered Athenian general Alcibiades, defied the Thirty Tyrants in order to bury his body

770 **Alceste** Alcestis was so devoted to her husband that she chose to die in his place

771 **Omer ... Penalopee** Penelope remained faithful to her husband, Odysseus, throughout his long absence, resisting and outwitting all suitors; her story is told by the ancient Greek writer Homer in his *Odyssey*

773 **Pardee** indeed

Laodomya when Laodamia's husband Protesilaus was killed at Troy, she voluntarily went with him to the underworld

776 **Porcia** Portia's worry about her husband Brutus led her to kill herself by swallowing hot coals

778 **To whom ... yive** to whom she had given her whole heart

779 **The parfit ... Arthemesie** the perfect wifeliness of Artemisia. Artemisia was so devoted to Mausolus, her husband, that when he died she built a tomb for him, so magnificent that it became one of the seven wonders of the world

780 **Barbarie** heathendom

781 **Teuta** Teuta was queen of Illyria in the third century BC. She was famed for her chastity and appears not to have married

783 **Bilyea** Bilia, wife of Duillius, was best known for putting up with her husband's bad breath, allegedly saying 'I thought the mouths of all men smelled like that'

784 **Rodogone** Rhodogune, daughter of the Persian king Darius, killed one of her servants for trying to persuade her to marry again

Valeria Valeria refused to remarry after the death of her husband

LINES 785–826   **Arveragus returns home and tells Dorigen that she must keep her promise to Aurelius**

When Arveragus returns home he finds Dorigen weeping and she tells him about her promise through her tears. 'Is that all, Dorigen?' he asks cheerfully. 'Let sleeping dogs lie. It might all turn out well yet'. But he insists that she must keep her promise, for 'a promise is the highest thing that one may keep'. However, he too then bursts into tears and makes Dorigen swear that she will never tell another living soul about what she is about to do. The Franklin interrupts his tale once more, addressing those who might be questioning Arveragus's judgement, urging them not to jump to conclusions before the end of the tale.

Ancient history may have demanded that raped wives commit suicide but Arveragus is not such a man. We now hear him speak for the first time in the tale: 'Is ther oght elles, Dorigen, but this?' (line 797). His calm, measured, even 'freendly' (line 795), response is in stark contrast to the continual noisy grief of his wife and Aurelius, though Arveragus too bursts into tears once he has reassured Dorigen (line 808). It is a display of the suffering kind of patience he swore he would show when he first got married. However, he also promised that he would not issue commands to his wife and is now doing exactly that, using expressions such as 'Ye shul'(line 802) and 'I yow forbede' (line 809). **Courtly love** may be a nice game but in the end male dominance reasserts itself. Illusion, however, is still present as Arveragus instructs his wife to feign cheerfulness and to tell no-one else of her promise, upon 'peyne of deeth' (line 809) and 'whil thee lasteth lyf ne breeth' (line 810). The 'freendly' tone has become sinister. By the end of the passage Dorigen is simply obeying orders and the whole focus is on Arveragus. 'As I may best, I wol my wo endure' (line 812) he says, as he sends his wife off to be raped. The patience of Arveragus is offering a way out of the dilemma but there is no mention of Dorigen's feelings.

786 **Purposinge** intending

790 **And she gan ... moore** and she began to cry even harder

794 **It nedeth ... namoore** I don't need to repeat it to you again

795 **chiere** expression

freendly wise friendly fashion

796 **yow devise** describe to you

797 **oght elles** anything else

798–9 **God helpe me ... wille** God help me indeed! This is already too much, even if it were God's will

800 **lat slepen that is stille** let sleeping dogs lie

801 **paraventure** perhaps

802 **Ye shul ... fay** you shall keep your promise, by my faith!

803–6 **For God ... save** for as surely as I hope God will have mercy on me, the great love I have for you means that I would rather be stabbed than that you should fail to keep and maintain your promise

808 **brast anon to wepe** burst into tears

810 **whil thee lasteth lyf ne breeth** while you live

811–14 **To no wight ... gesse** tell no-one what has happened – I will bear my troubles as best I can – and don't have a sorrowful expression which might make people suspect or think badly of you

815 **cleped** called

819 **they ne wiste** they did not know

820 **He nolde ... entente** he would not tell his plan to anyone

821 **heep** lot

ywis indeed

822 **holden** consider

lewed stupid

823 **jupartie** danger

824 **Herkneth ... crie** listen to the story before you condemn her

825 **yow semeth** you expect

826 **demeth** judge

LINES 827–72   Aurelius is moved by Dorigen's weeping and by the honourable behaviour of Arveragus. He therefore releases her from her vow

Aurelius encounters Dorigen in the busiest street in the town and asks her where she is going. She replies that her husband has ordered her to keep her promise and that she was on her way to do so. Aurelius is amazed and feels pity both for the weeping Dorigen and for Arveragus, who would rather send his wife to meet another man than have her break her word. On reflection, he would rather sacrifice his desire than commit an offence against such generosity of spirit and nobility. 'Madam,' he says, 'tell your husband that I would rather suffer eternally than destroy the love you two have for one another. I release you from your vow.' He then takes his leave, declaring that she is the truest and best wife he has ever known, but warns women to be careful what they promise. Thus, he concludes, a squire is as capable of a noble act as a knight.

> The final meeting between Aurelius and Dorigen is not a tryst in a romantic garden as he had intended. The absurdities of **courtly love** reach their peak as the weeping 'lady' encounters her 'loving servant' (who has, incidentally, been stalking her) in the middle of the high street, and tells him that they are about to have sex with the permission of her husband. It is not surprising that Aurelius 'gan wondren on this cas' (line 842). He is moved to pity, allegedly by Dorigen's tears and by the 'generosity' of her husband. Dorigen's obvious reluctance has not, however, had any effect on him before and it is clear that it is the 'franchise' and 'gentillesse' (line 852) of Arveragus that moves him to pity, or possibly even to compete. Dorigen is no longer the issue. She is reduced to being a pretty warning to other women to beware what they promise (lines 869–70). Aurelius now has other concerns. The man who had wanted to rival Arveragus in love now wants to rival him in 'gentillesse'. Thus, one man's 'generosity' leads to the 'generosity' of another man.

827 **highte** was called

828 **On Dorigen ... amorous** who was in love with Dorigen

829 **Of aventure** by chance

830 **Amidde** in the middle of

quikkest strete busiest street

831 **bown** prepared

832 **hight** promised

833–5 **And he was ... place** and he was also on his way to the garden; for he watched intently and knew whenever she left her house to go anywhere

836 **of aventure or grace** by chance or design

837 **And he saleweth ... entente** and he greeted her in a state of happy expectation

840 **bad** ordered

841 **My trouthe for to holde** to keep my promise

842 **Aurelius ... cas** Aurelius was astonished at this turn in events

846 **hight** promised

847 **So looth ... trouthe** he was so unwilling that his wife should break her promise

848 **he caughte of this greet routhe** he felt great pity at this

850–2 **That fro ... gentillesse** that he would prefer not to have his desire fulfilled than to commit such a terrible, ignoble and miserable offence against generosity and courtesy

857–8 **That him ...trouthe** that he would prefer to be humiliated (which would be a pity) than that you should break your promise to me

860 **departe** break up

861–3 **I yow ... heerbiforn** Madam, I release into your own keeping every oath and promise which you made to me before, all fully repaid

865–6 **I shal yow never repreve / Of no biheste** I shall never reproach you for any promise

867 **As of** from

871 **doon a gentil dede** perform a noble act

872 **withouten drede** doubtless

LINES 873–84   Dorigen and Arveragus are overjoyed and live happily ever after

Dorigen thanks Aurelius on her knees and goes home to her husband, telling him everything that has happened. Arveragus's joy, declares the

Franklin, would be impossible to describe. He and Dorigen live the rest of their lives in bliss, with Arveragus treating her like a queen, while she was true to him ever afterwards.

> Dorigen, who had once been viewed as the courtly lady, remote and unapproachable, is last seen on her knees thanking the man who reduced her to misery, returning to the man who sent her to endure still more. The Franklin rushes over the details, presenting the typically happy ending we might have found in any **romance**: 'soverein blisse ... for everemoore' (lines 880–3), with Arveragus treating Dorigen like a queen (line 882). But this was not just 'any romance', it had challenged the **stereotypes** and attempted to create a new kind of relationship between men and women based on equality. The return to this traditional, exaggerated vocabulary, indicates that the attempt has been a failure. Being treated like a queen may sound grand, but it is an indication that the woman is no longer an equal and has been pushed back into her stereotypical role where she can do no harm.

873 **upon hir knees al bare** on her bare knees

874 **fare** gone

876 **be ye siker** you can be sure
     apayd pleased

878 **endite** write

880 **In soverein ... lyf** live the rest of their lives in supreme happiness

884 **namoore** no more

LINES 885–912   Aurelius is unable to pay the clerk all he owes

Aurelius curses the day that he was born: his effort has been for nothing and he now owes the clerk 1,000 pounds in gold. It seems that he will have to sell his inheritance and become a beggar, somewhere far away where he will not bring shame upon his family. His one hope is that the clerk will be merciful and allow him to pay his debt in instalments. With a heavy heart, he fetches 500 pounds of gold from his chest and approaches the clerk. He promises him that the rest of the debt will be paid, claiming that he has never in his life broken his word.

Dorigen may have been safely consigned back to the world of **romance** but Aurelius is facing the very unromantic prospect of having to pay his debts. The **courtly lover** who had earlier declared, 'Fy on a thousand pound!' saying that he would give the whole world to win his lady (lines 555–7), now finds that his declarations are slightly problematic in the real world. The language of love and knightly service is reduced to a business context as Aurelius begs the clerk for 'grace' (line 894) and permission to pay in instalments, appealing to his 'grete curteisye' (line 897) not to call in the debt at once. 'Trouthe' which, according to Arveragus had been 'the hyeste thing that man may kepe' (line 807), is reduced to a debtor's word that he is good for the money.

885   **that his cost hath al forlorn**   who has completely wasted his money
887   **bihighte**   promised
888   **of wighte**   in weight
889   **philosophre**   scientist
890–1   **I se ... selle**   It seems that I'm completely ruined. I must sell my inheritance
894   **But I ... grace**   unless I can obtain more mercy from him
895–6   **I wole ... paye**   I will attempt to pay him on certain days every year
897   **curteisye**   courtesy
899   **cofre**   chest
902   **bisecheth**   begs
      gentillesse   generosity of spirit
903   **dayes of the remenaunt**   additional time to pay the balance
904   **make avaunt**   boast
905   **I failled ... yit**   I have never yet failed to keep a promise
906   **sikerly**   without doubt
      quit   paid
907–8   **howevere ... bare**   even if I have to go begging in my bare tunic
909–10   **But wolde ... me**   but would you be willing, with proper security, to grant me a respite of two or three years?

LINES 913–48   The clerk releases Aurelius from his bargain

'Have I not kept my side of the bargain, and have you not had your lady?' demands the clerk. Aurelius tells him the whole story: the noble nature of Arveragus, the sorrow of Dorigen, and his own generosity in sending her back to her husband. The clerk acknowledges that both men have displayed great magnanimity and swears that he will not be outdone. He accordingly releases Aurelius from his debt and rides away.

Aurelius is clearly impressed by the 'gentillesse' of Arveragus, naming him first and taking three lines to explain his generosity. He is keen to speak of Dorigen too, though the claim that she would have rather died than sleep with him and in fact had never even heard of illusion is not borne out by the tale. Dorigen had no designs on Aurelius, but to exonerate her from all responsibility is to reduce her from a rational agent to a mere doll. In fact, this is effectively how we see her last, reduced to the inanimate role in a game of male ping pong as she is propelled from one man to the other: 'And right as frely as he sente hire me, / As frely sente I hire to him ageyn' (lines 932–3). The men have taken control and now the magician wants to play too: he also shall perform a 'gentil' deed. *Gentillesse*, that great word in medieval chivalry, has become a little grubby along the way. It is capable of describing more noble deeds than this but, in the great mess that the characters have created for themselves, it is perhaps as much as we can expect.

913 **sobrely** gravely

923 **of gentillesse** on account of his noble nature

929 **levere hadde** would rather

930 **She nevere ... apparence** she had never before heard of such illusions

932–3 **And right ... ageyn** and with as much generosity as he showed in sending her to me, I generously sent her back to him again

934 **This al and som** this is the whole story

935 **Leeve** dear

937 **Everich ... oother** each of you behaved nobly towards the other

938–40 **But God ... drede** but God forbid, in his glory, that even a scholar like me shouldn't be able to perform a noble deed as well as any of you, and that's a fact

942 **As thou ... ground** as if you had only just entered the world

945 **travaille** labour

946 **Thou hast ...vitaille** you have done enough in providing me with food

LINES 949–52   The Franklin asks the company a question

The tale has come to an end but the Franklin has one last thing to ask: of all the people in his story, who displayed the greatest generosity? He himself has nothing more to add but it is a question he feels should be answered before the company rides any further.

> In the sources for this tale an answer is provided but Chaucer chooses not to give us one. Instead this is a tale which begins with a 'solution' and ends with a question. It is not, as some critics have suggested, the conclusion to a marriage debate, rather it has taken the possible conclusion and shown it to be problematic. A well-brought up knight and lady deciding to have a marriage based on equality may seem ideal, but the tale shows us what happens when this is attempted in the 'real' world. Medieval society has established roles that men and women are expected to play and equality does not fit comfortably with these. It is a grand experiment: what happens when you take the **utopian** vision of marriage and try to make it work in the fourteenth century? The result is a mess with the Franklin attempting to push characters back into their pigeonholes to live happily ever after. Such an ending is the final illusion in the tale. But Chaucer does not end with that. He leaves us with a question, not an answer. Of course, it is typical of the Franklin that it is the wrong question, but at least it is clear that this tale is not meant to leave us thinking that all is well with the world.

949 **Lordinges** gentlemen

950 **Which was ... yow** who was the most generous, do you think?

951 **er that ye ferther wende** before you go any further

952 **kan** know

PART THREE

CRITICAL APPROACHES

NARRATIVE TECHNIQUE

All the pilgrims in *The Canterbury Tales* are described with enthusiasm by Chaucer the narrator. The narrator character is a happy, rather innocent individual who is terribly impressed by the people on the pilgrimage. Almost everyone is declared to be a 'good fellow', from the drunken Miller, who is fond of breaking down doors with his head, to the homicidal Shipman. There is very rarely any direct criticism but this does not mean that the characters are not to be criticised. Instead there is very often implied condemnation at the very point at which the narrator is most complimentary. For example, the star-struck narrator may be deeply in awe of the table manners of the Prioress, but the reader knows that more is to be expected from a nun than keeping her fingers out of the sauce dip. This technique of using exuberant praise to undermine a character is known as **Chaucerian irony**. Of course, there are also occasions when praise is simply praise, so it is up to the reader to decide what is ironic and what is not. With some characters this is straightforward: the poor Parson who takes care of the people with no thought for his own welfare can safely be called a good man; the enthusiasm shown for the overweight and overindulgent Friar, on the other hand, is bound to be ironic. The Franklin, however, is not such a clear-cut case.

CHARACTERISATION

THE FRANKLIN

There has been a great deal of debate about the character of the Franklin. Some critics view him as a warm and generous man, learned and tolerant, even a 'Santa Claus' figure (Donaldson); an ideal pilgrim presenting us with an ideal world (Kittredge). Other critics take an entirely different view: to these he is a pleasure-loving upstart who only wants to impress

(Robertson); or, at best, a naïve country squire unable to handle his courtly material (Howard).

The most consistent accusation against the Franklin is that he is a social climber: one of those who became rich quick at the end of the fourteenth century and who now lay on opulent feasts with no idea of how things really should be done. Such a criticism arises partly from the fact that the term 'franklin' is not a precise one. However, it is clear that franklins were country gentlemen, frequently land owning and very wealthy. They were not of noble birth but they were minor gentry and as such were neither upstarts nor *nouveaux riches*. Such men could hold prominent positions and Chaucer's Franklin has held many of them: member of parliament, justice of the peace, sheriff and auditor. Those who wish to present the Franklin as an ideal point out that Chaucer himself had been many of these things; those who wish to condemn the Franklin refer to the sheer number of positions as evidence of his grasping and over-ambitious nature.

It is true that the character of the Franklin reveals a certain amount of ambition, for his son if not for himself. Interrupting the young Squire, the Franklin bemoans his son's behaviour, a young man who would rather gamble and talk to servants than learn about 'gentillesse' (line 22). This is the cause of great grief to the Franklin, for 'gentillesse', noble behaviour, is his great love. It is a word that is repeated many times in both the prologue and tale. The Franklin prides himself on such behaviour and the idea is implicit throughout his portrait in the *General Prologue*. His is a household fit for any nobleman, where there is abundance of food and drink, where the table always stands ready, and, above all, where everything has to be done right:

> Wo was his cook but if his sauce were
> Poynaunt and sharp, and redy al his geere
>
> (*The General Prologue*, lines 353–4)

This preoccupation with sauces, together with the fact that half of the portrait is given over to a description of food, has led many to accuse the Franklin of gluttony. The well-stocked cellar, the morning sop of wine, the partridges, the fish (especially the *luce*, or pike), all appear in medieval **satires** on gluttony. And yet there is no mention here of the nausea, vomiting and excretion which inevitably follow all this food in the satires.

Instead, the Franklin is described as having a 'sangwin' disposition (*The General Prologue*, line 335): a healthy and generous nature. Medieval science divided people into four types according to the preponderance of fluids known as 'humours' in the body. The sanguine person was thought to be dominated by blood and all the medieval texts agree that this is an excellent body type, denoting a person much given to joy and laughter, enjoying the company of the opposite sex, slow to anger, of strong constitution, and of pleasant appearance.

The good living, in both senses, of the Franklin is further emphasised by his 'seasonable' diet, the practice of varying one's eating habits in accordance with the seasons being wholeheartedly approved of by medieval manuals on health. Thus, the catalogue of dishes in the Franklin's portrait may be lengthy but the whole description is bound up with an idea of good health, fine living and generosity. In short, he is a veritable Saint Julian (*The General Prologue*, line 343), the patron saint of hospitality, so called because he entertained Christ himself in his home.

He is also, however, 'Epicurus owene sone' (*The General Prologue*, line 339) which is a far more alarming **metaphor**. The ancient philosopher Epicurus was associated in the Middle Ages with the belief that gratification of the senses was the highest pleasure, and the text at this point repeats the word *delit* ('delight') for emphasis. And yet, this is not a wholly accurate account of the teaching of Epicurus. He did believe that pleasure was the beginning and end of the good life but he also believed that it was not possible to live pleasurably without also living wisely and righteously. To be an Epicurean is not, therefore, a bad thing in itself. What is worrying in this description is the fact that virtue is not mentioned and pleasure has too much prominence.

The Franklin is not a bad man; he is not a glutton or a social climber. He is a well-intentioned country landowner who tries to do his best and has a fondness for the 'higher' things in life. He does not quite fully understand these 'higher' things: philosophy is half digested and he is discourteous to both the Squire and his own son in the very act of praising good manners. What he does understand is the importance of a good table and so he does this to excess, demanding excellence at all times.

This combination of good intentions, incomprehension and excess are what characterise the Franklin. He is not a noble knight: his 'love' is a piece of wine-soaked bread; his gentleman's purse is like creamy morning milk; and the only person he terrorises is his cook. With his white beard and hair and rosy complexion he is compared to a daisy. It is not the grandest of flowers but it is still a positive image, a little 'eye of the day', a little sun.

In short, the Franklin is exactly what Chaucer declares him to be: a 'worthy vavasour'. (See also Language & Style, on The Franklin as Narrator.)

DORIGEN

We first encounter Dorigen as the typical courtly lady of medieval **romance**. She is the unattainable beauty whom the knight must serve faithfully before she can be won. She is a **stereotype**, an ideal of femininity, and it is significant that she has a husband in our tale long before she has a name. She is simply the ideal married woman: beautiful, noble, reserved and wedded to a knight as well born, virtuous and courteous as herself.

The two of them surmount the tale like the figures on a wedding cake: images of perfection and unity. This is the point at which most medieval courtly ladies disappear, or are at least subsumed by their husband's identity, but Dorigen is going to be permitted a real life, based on equality, in which she can act and think for herself. She is even given a name, Dorigen, albeit a name which comes with the tag, 'his wyf' (line 143). The lady is being released from the tower and is free to make her own choices.

Having been relieved of the role of courtly lady, the first thing Dorigen decides is that she will become a tragic heroine. Arveragus is away and we hear that his wife, 'moorneth, waketh, waileth, fasteth, pleyneth' (line 147). In fact, Dorigen possibly spends more time in tears than any other heroine in English literature. She begins weeping at line 145 and is still distraught almost 700 lines later. Of course, there is the occasional respite during which time Dorigen stops crying long enough to get herself into trouble, but it is significant that her favourite word appears to be 'allas'. It punctuates her speech (e.g. lines 181, 670, 683,

693, 733, 757, 791) and the very last words we hear from her are an emphatic, 'allas, allas!' (line 841). Her grief is highly dramatic and also self-indulgent. This is how noble women behave 'whan hem liketh' (line 146), says the Franklin revealingly.

We should not assume that Dorigen is play-acting all the time: her love for her husband and her grief at his absence are genuine. However, she cannot resist making a drama out of a crisis, literally so in her forty-eight-hour marathon list of the women of history who chose death before dishonour. The account concludes mischievously:

> Thus pleyned Dorigen a day or tweye,
> Purposinge evere that she wolde deye.
> But nathelees, upon the thridde night,
> Hoom cam Arveragus … (lines 785–8)

Her great resolve to die has still got nowhere by the third night. Not that Dorigen should die. No-one even considers it as a possibility except her. It is just that, faced with a problem, she seizes the opportunity to see herself as Lucretia or Penelope or even all the daughters of Phidon. It is perhaps the response of a woman for whom the stereotypes have been removed. She is not to be the haughty lady or the subordinate wife: these roles were swept away at the beginning and a new role as equal was introduced. However, Dorigen seems unclear how to act in a role that the Franklin could not even adequately describe. She therefore latches on to other stereotypes: tragic heroine, virgin martyr and, worst of all, courtly mistress.

When she is approached by Aurelius, Dorigen has no intention whatsoever of becoming his lover. As she flatteringly puts it later, she would rather die. Her response to him is an unambiguous 'no', except for the part about the rocks which she adds 'in pley' (line 316). It seems like a fine time for our lachrymose heroine to develop a sense of humour, but Dorigen is not, in fact, joking Aurelius out of his folly as some critics suggest. If so, her reference to husbands enjoying their wives' bodies, which follows immediately afterwards, would undo her good work. The 'pley' is not, in the end, about Aurelius. It is about Dorigen. Faced with an ardent suitor, this newly created, entirely equal, medieval wife is not sure what to do. She knows that she wants to reject him but there is no model for how this should be done, just as there is now no model for anything in her life. She therefore momentarily adopts the role of disdainful courtly mistress to Aurelius's humble servant of love and orders him to remove all the rocks in the sea. This, she thinks, will get rid of him, but she is wrong.

In fact, Dorigen is wrong about a number of things in the tale. She even tackles God on the small matter of the existence of evil in the world. It is a legitimate enough question, but the interesting thing is that Dorigen does not care to wait around for an answer. She knows that the 'clerkes' will have 'argumentz' (lines 213–14) but she does not want to listen. All she can think of is Arveragus and utters the stubborn, foot-stamping declaration, 'kepe my lord! This is my conclusion' (line 217). This hard-headedness is reflected in the **imagery** associated with Dorigen. The unyielding rocks are the focus of her fears and rock becomes her **symbol**. Her inconsolable mind is compared to stone being chipped at by a sculptor as her friends try to comfort her (lines 157–63) and it is no accident that she is 'astoned' (line 667) when Aurelius reveals that the task is completed. Even her name is associated with rocks, the similar sounding Droguen being a prominent rock in the Penmarch area.

In the end, when creating a new way of life, something more flexible than stone is required, and a heroine more adaptable than Dorigen is needed. In the course of the tale she falls apart. The proud lady of the tale's opening has become a hysterical, illogical victim by the time she reaches her catalogue of happy suicides. Her free will is handed back to her husband as she surrenders herself to the role of subordinate wife, and the last time we see her she is on her knees before Aurelius. We do, however, hear of her one last time as the Franklin relates that she and Arveragus lived happily ever after:

> He cherisseth hire as though she were a queene,
> And she was to him trewe for everemoore. (lines 882–3)

Dorigen has been placed back in a role that the Middle Ages knew how to deal with: the excessive and ultimately meaningless 'woman as queen'. It is important to note, though, that Dorigen does not behave like a queen, she is merely treated like one, for her role is no longer to behave like anything. She has become passive and her entire personality has been reduced to her sexual honour. The attempt to create a new wifely role has failed and the stereotypes have reasserted themselves. It is not clear what the answer to the Franklin's final question, 'Which was the mooste fre?', should be, but it is clear that were we to ask 'Who was the least free?' the answer would be Dorigen.

AURELIUS

Aurelius enters *The Franklin's Tale* amidst a stream of praise. He is,

> Yong, strong, right vertuous, and riche, and wys,
> And wel biloved, and holden in greet prys. (lines 261–2)

The Franklin cannot resist heaping yet more adjectives upon this fine young man, descending into a breathless repetition of 'and' as he adds more to the list. Nor is this surprising, for Aurelius is introduced as an ideal. Like Dorigen and Arveragus, he is first presented as a **stereotype**, in his case a perfect squire, a noble young man in training to become a knight. As he sings and dances his way into the tale he is compared to the flourishing, beautiful month of May (lines 255–6). In fact, in medieval picture calendars May was often presented as a young, brightly dressed squire. It is as though this young man has just walked out of the picture and into the tale.

May was also associated in the Middle Ages with lovers and our calendar boy is indeed 'servant to Venus' (line 265). All the medieval books of **courtly love**, all the manuals on how to be a noble lover, are used here to form the character of Aurelius. Like Dorigen, however, he has a tendency to play his part to excess. He knows all the vocabulary, begging his lady for 'grace' and 'mercy', urging her to 'reweth' upon him, talking constantly of his 'peynes smerte'. He loves, pines, suffers and wastes away, and never insults his lady by doing any of these things for less than two years at a time. He declares his death to be imminent more than a dozen times in the course of the narrative and is only ten lines into his first conversation with Dorigen before he is asking to be buried at her feet (line 304). Rejection finds him declaring that he must 'dye of sodeyn deth horrible' (line 358), though in fact he goes off to lick his wounds for another two years. Even the Franklin eventually seems to lose patience with Aurelius as he faints with the pain of unrequited love: 'Lete I this woful creature lie' he says, 'Chese he, for me, wheither he wol live or die' (lines 413–14).

The noble aspects of courtly love disappear amidst Aurelius's excessive and unappealing attempts to be the ideal courtly lover. In spite of knowing all the rules and following them to the letter he is not the greatest servant Venus has ever had. He is not a Lancelot or a Tristram, the best the narrator can do for him is to compare him to Pamphilus (line 438), a perfectly commendable lover in his way but not one of the literary greats: a medieval audience as much as a modern one is likely to have asked, 'Who?' Aurelius fares no better with any of the other **similes** in the tale. Love does not ennoble him, it makes him act like a Fury (line 278) and pine the way Echo did for Narcissus (lines 279–80). It is interesting to note that both Echo and the Furies are female. Courtly love, which was designed to make a knight even more of a man and spur him on to even more noble acts, has emasculated Aurelius and reduced him to a pining girl and a complete monstrosity.

And monstrous he does indeed become. The 'fressh', 'joly' squire of the tale's opening is lurking in doorways by the end, watching Dorigen's house and aware of her movements at all times. He still hides behind the mask of his courtliness but the speech in which he tells her that the rocks are gone is menacing and coercive. He will not, in the end, be content so long as he can die at her feet. He wants Dorigen's body, not as some act of courtly 'mercy' but as his right. Courtly love belongs to a **romance** world of which Aurelius is no longer a part at the end of the tale. His plans for a sexual encounter with the woman of his dreams in the garden of all romantic authors' dreams is swept aside and replaced by an uncomfortable encounter with a half crazed woman in the middle of the street, discussing the mechanics of who has given permission for whom to have sex with whom. It is not promising, but from this there is a sudden revelation. The man who has been begging from the beginning for courtly 'mercy' suddenly feels pity of his own. His heart, the focus of much pain and bleeding up until now, suddenly feels 'greet routhe' (line 848) and Aurelius is able to think of Dorigen and Arveragus for the first time without being intimately involved. All the over-dramatic courtly language which had characterised his speech disappears in his final conversations with Dorigen and the clerk as, for the first time in the tale, he performs a truly 'gentil' act. It is not, to answer the Franklin's final question, the most generous and 'gentil' act in the world but he is at least no longer a monster. He is not even a romance hero. Instead he realises for the first time that he is a 'squier … [who can] doon a gentil dede' (line 871).

ARVERAGUS

Like the others, Arveragus appears in the tale as a **stereotype** long before he is given a name. He is a knight and we first see him wooing Dorigen as the books tell us a knight should: performing chivalric deeds and offering himself with the utmost humility. Of course, he suffers 'wo, …peyne, and … distresse' (line 65) but the Franklin limits himself to three **synonyms**, and it is clear that this is love sickness as it should be, and not the over-dramatic mortal illness of Aurelius. So far, it is a conventional picture of proper knightly conduct. However, he then declares to Dorigen that he:

> Ne sholde upon him take no maistrie
>
> Again hir wil, ne kithe hire jalousie,
>
> But hire obeye, and folwe hir wil in al,
>
> As any lovere to his lady shal (lines 75–8)

This is an unexpected turn of events: to treat a wife as though she were still his honoured lady. The only thing he asks is that it should seem to the world as though he were still in charge. Thus, we have here the basic parts of Arveragus's character. He is a good knight, forward thinking even, though with a concern for appearances which will be with him until the end of the tale.

Unlike the others, Arveragus could not be called excessive, but he does have a tendency to stick too much to the letter of things. From the beginning his every action displays a meticulous concern for two ideals: 'gentillesse' (line 82) and 'degree' (line 80). 'Gentillesse' prompts him to put his relationship with his wife on a more equal footing, but 'degree', his concern for his social status, causes him to keep this secret and to go off after only a year to seek 'worshipe and honour' (line 139) in England. Arveragus is a good knight but he is also a bit of a stickler and these two aspects compete in his character, most obviously so when Dorigen tells him about her hasty promise to Aurelius. The Arveragus who keeps to the rules tells his wife to 'let sleeping dogs lie', and informs her that she must keep her promise. He may burst into tears but he also utters that immortal line, 'Trouthe is the hyeste thing that man may kepe' (line 807). It is an excellent saying and fit for any chivalrous knight, band of warriors, or medieval civil servant. The problem is that it may not be wholly appropriate for a grief-stricken man whose wife has just made a very rash promise. 'Trouthe' may well be the *highest* thing but it is significantly not the *only* thing. However, Arveragus is just as adamant as Dorigen can be and keeps to the letter of the law as he sees it. Nor is it just Dorigen's word of honour that is at stake, for Aurelius too has made a promise. Back at the beginning of the tale when he married Dorigen we were told that he 'suffrance hire bihight' (line 116) and it is his own oath of patience as much as adherence to Dorigen's rash promise that guides him here.

To answer the Franklin's final question, this is not a 'fre' act, it is a tight-lipped, law-abiding response to a problem. Arveragus had tried to break through traditional constraints in his marriage to Dorigen but even here he had wanted still to look like a traditional medieval man, keeping to the social rules. This is exactly what he does in the end as he seizes upon 'truth' as a certainty in the midst of a moral mess and orders Dorigen, upon pain of death, to keep her promise and to keep her mouth shut. Just like Dorigen and Aurelius, Arveragus has his limitations and a fondness for illusion. He is far less theatrical than the others but he is also ultimately playing a role. Nevertheless, he is still a man who had attempted to live differently, who had at some level desired equality with his wife and who had promised to live patiently with her. The experiment has not been a success but the spirit of generosity and toleration which motivated it survives to the end of the tale. Dorigen is no longer its beneficiary, being bundled off as almost an embarrassment to the Franklin, but there is something in Arveragus, flawed as he is, that is still commendable. In the midst of the great moral mess that is the end of *The Franklin's Tale*, Arveragus's willingness to suffer is the one bright spot. Dazzling it is not, but amongst characters whose refusal to endure anything patiently had caused all the problems in the first place, it is enough of a spark to set off a modest display of tolerance and *gentillesse* all round.

THE CLERK

The clerk is never given a name in the tale and so it might be expected that he would be even more of a **stereotype** than the other characters: a wizened old magician, lurking in the darkness and waving his wand. In fact, the opposite is true: he is young, successful and professional. He does have an uncanny knowledge of why Aurelius and his brother are in Orleans and can conjure up wonders of various kinds, but he does not otherwise act like a magician. In spite of the fact that he has the most dramatic role in the tale, he seems to lead a very ordinary life, albeit a very comfortable one:

> So wel arrayed hous as ther was oon
> Aurelius in his lyf saugh nevere noon (lines 515–16)

His magic is practised in his study, not on some desolate hillside, and he has a decided fondness for his 'soper' (line 538), a liking for food that emerges again at the end of the tale when he declares that the 'vitals' he has been given are payment enough. This, however, is the only distinguishing feature of a character who is otherwise detached and unemotional.

He makes no comment while Aurelius's brother weeps for his dead friends (lines 509–10) and his only remark about the transfixed Aurelius is the wry observation that, 'Thise amorous folk somtime moote han hir reste' (line 546). However, he has quietly and calmly brought Aurelius to the point where he is willing to offer anything for his services. He begins by casually, and apparently effortlessly, stating the nature of their business, and then shows them some pretty illusions culminating in the dance of Dorigen and the squire. But this is not allowed to last long, it is a mere tantalising taste of what he can do. He claps his hands and at once, 'Al oure revel was ago' (line 532). Aurelius is hooked and willing to offer the whole world if that's what it takes. In fact, what it does take is 1,000 pounds in weight of pure gold, a huge sum equivalent to millions of pounds in money. The clerk is nothing if not an astute businessman.

The nature of his magic reinforces the idea that what is at stake is a clear-cut deal rather than the black arts. There is nothing dark or sinister about the man, and his magic is the sort that comes from books, steeped in the scientific terminology of medieval astrology. It remains, however, illusion and this is what he has in common with the other characters, all of whom are tied up in their own illusions. The fundamental difference is that for the magician it is only a way of making money. His final act is, as the Franklin would say, 'fre' but it does not have all the resonances of the word. His generosity is of a financial kind and there is even something a touch mathematical about the way he figures himself into the final equation:

> Thou art a squire, and he is a knight;
>
> But God forbede, for his blisful might,
>
> But if a clerk koude doon a gentil dede (lines 937–9)

He calculates the final bill, 'craft' and 'travaille' (line 945), parts plus labour, but remains supremely unemotional to the end, dismissing the debt and leaving with what sounds anachronistically like 'Have a nice day!' (line 947).

THEMES

MEDIEVAL MARRIAGE & COURTLY LOVE

Marriage in the Middle Ages, especially amongst the aristocracy, was not always a matter of individual choice. Families frequently arranged marriages for economic, political or social reasons, and while it was of course preferable and far easier to arrange a union between willing parties, it did not always work out that way. Noble families, in particular, viewed marriage as an important way of forming alliances, increasing their power or adding to their wealth, and this no doubt resulted in some reluctant brides and bridegrooms. Children could be betrothed by their families even before they were born, and girls as young as twelve or boys as young as fourteen could be married. A married man would at least become head of his own household but a woman merely passed from being under the control of her father to being under the control of her husband. She was expected to obey him in all things, her own desires being second to his. In law she was not his equal but his property and as such had no rights of her own.

The medieval idea of love, on the other hand, was very different. **Courtly love** emerged in France in the early Middle Ages and was the subject of a great deal of poetry. It was a code of love in which the lady has all the power, holding the fate of her would-be lover in her hand. She is not required to accept any man and is a harsh and unforgiving mistress, setting her loyal knight difficult and often arbitrary tasks. However, these tasks are a means for the man to achieve perfection. Love is a source of inspiration, spurring him on to heroic deeds that will help him reach his full potential as both a man and a warrior. The woman does not develop. Her role is that of adored object, preferably adored from afar. The knight was expected to worship the lady, who was frequently married, regarding her as the **image** of unattainable perfection.

The relationship between a man and a woman before marriage is, therefore, very different from the relationship they have after marriage. Power swings radically away from the woman and into the hands of the man, leaving our mighty, disdainful lady a powerless piece of property. This is the situation that Chaucer examines in *The Franklin's Tale*. Everything begins in the traditional manner with the knight and lady following all the conventions of courtly love in their courtship. She is the remote figure all the poets say she must be, only giving in to her suitor 'atte laste' (line 66), after he has performed 'many a labour, many a greet emprise' (line 60), and has shown himself to have suffered 'penaunce' (line 68) with humility as a loyal servant should. However, the minute the lady decides to take this man as her husband, the power becomes his:

> ... prively she fil of his accord
> To take him for hir housbonde and hir lord (lines 69–70)

'Lord' and 'husband': the two words go together, for a woman's husband is by nature her superior.

However, this arrangement is challenged in *The Franklin's Tale*. The knight says that he does not want the traditional role. Instead he wants his courtly lady to retain her power and hands back the 'maistrie' (line 75) to her. This word, 'maistrie', is a very important one to Chaucer. One of his other pilgrims, the Wife of Bath, has already told a story in which it is claimed that what women want most in the whole world is 'maistrie' over their husbands, and to prove it her tale is about a knight whose ugly old wife becomes beautiful and faithful as soon as he surrenders 'maistrie' to her. That is where *The Wife of Bath's Tale* ends, but it is where our tale begins. Chaucer is trying out the experiment offered by the other tale: what happens once the social order has been rearranged in a marriage?

Well, what happens in *The Franklin's Tale* is complete disaster. It all ends in tears, literally, as fourteenth-century husbands might have expected it would. Dorigen, left to her own devices, gets herself into an intolerable situation. No longer the silent partner in a marriage, she gives her word, her 'trouthe', to another man with dreadful consequences. While it is true that her husband respects her enough to take her promise seriously, something he is not required to do under law, it is the last time that Dorigen will give her word to anyone as she is told henceforth to be silent 'up peyne of deeth' (line 809). Her husband reclaims the authority that he had given to her in the beginning and tells her what to do. Nor is it gentle advice: 'Ye shul youre trouthe holden, by my fay!' (line 802), he declares.

The woman who had been begged for pity earlier in the tale has become the object of the men's pity. Male power reasserts itself as the Franklin clears everything up neatly for a happy ending, but it cannot involve the earlier attempt at a marriage of equality, for that attempt has failed. Instead, there is a return to a far more traditional view of marriage where the woman is cherished 'as though she were a queene' (line 882). It is ultimately a powerless role, an equal wife having far more status than any cherished queen. This, however, is the status quo that allows them to lead the rest of their lives in 'soverein blisse' (line 880). It is an interesting choice of words, for if Dorigen is indeed the queen then Arveragus is her sovereign, and no doubt a happy one now that proper order has been restored.

It is not, however, a surprise that this relationship of mutual power fails, for it is difficult to change an institution if society does not change with it. While Arveragus was happy for his wife to be his equal, he did not want it to be publicly known that this was the case, demanding still 'the name of soveraineteee … for shame of his degree' (lines 79–80). The couple may have moved on but society is still demanding life by the old rules and it is difficult to change when everyone around wants things to remain as they are. Medieval society is not even capable of describing this new relationship, as the Franklin discovers to his cost. The end of the tale is thus a failure for this brave new world of marriage, but it is not a triumphant failure. No-one seems to glory in seeing Dorigen returned to a traditionally subordinate role. The Franklin certainly does not, rushing over the fate of his married couple in only six lines and declaring, 'Of thise two folk ye gete of me namoore' (line 884).

VIRTUE

Marriage is a central theme in *The Franklin's Prologue and Tale* but there is also an examination of moral qualities that goes beyond marriage. Three moral concepts are examined in detail: *trouthe, gentillesse* and *paciens.*

TROUTHE
Trouthe was a very important concept in the Middle Ages. The word means 'truth' but it is truth in all senses: being true to one's word, to one's self, to others and to the codes of medieval society. It is no surprise, therefore, to hear Arveragus declare that, 'Trouthe is the hyeste thing that man may kepe' (line 807). The word is central to *The Franklin's Tale* with each of the characters bound to at least one of the others by their plighted troth. It is the word used by Dorigen in her marriage vow to her husband (line 87); it is also the word she uses to Aurelius when she asks him to remove the rocks (line 326); it is the word Aurelius uses to seal his bargain with the clerk (line 559); it is the word Arveragus uses in sending Dorigen to keep her promise (line 806); and it is the word used when Aurelius promises to pay his debts at the end (line 905).

However, it is clear that there is a difference between the *trouthe* that forms part of Dorigen's loving agreement with her husband and the *trouthe* that Aurelius swears to the magician. The word begins as a lofty concept but is devalued in the course of the tale. The first time it is used it encompasses all the wider definitions of the word as Dorigen promises Arveragus faithfully, generously and courteously that she will be his wife. However, the next time she swears by *trouthe* it is a flippant remark to an unwanted suitor. Aurelius uses the word throughout to describe nothing more than his business dealings with the clerk. As for Arveragus, in spite of sounding very authoritative, he approaches the word like a legal agreement and ignores all the wider implications which would have to take into consideration the fact that Dorigen has already made a marriage vow to him, did not expect her task to be truly accepted, and would not be being true to herself in fulfilling such a rash promise. *Trouthe* therefore begins as a lofty concept and moves in a downward spiral until it is used merely to confirm Aurelius's ability to pay his debts in instalments. It cannot even be said that the idea of the sacred oath is what ultimately saves all the characters, for had each of them strictly kept their promise then Dorigen would have been raped, Arveragus would have been heartbroken, and Aurelius would have faced a life of crippling debt.

GENTILLESSE

The Franklin is very fond of the word *gentillesse*. It is used so much in his conversation with the Squire that the Host finally interrupts in exasperation, shouting 'Straw for your gentillesse!' (line 23). The Franklin apologises – and makes sure that the word appears in the very first line of his prologue. The Franklin's concern with the word is not surprising. It is a very important medieval term and is central to a number of *The Canterbury Tales*. It is not, however, easy to translate into modern English as it encompasses a number of moral qualities. The simplest translation is 'nobility' but it is a nobility that involves generosity, sympathy for others, graciousness, a sense of honour, and our old friend *trouthe*.

The prologue therefore begins with the assertion that the tale originated amongst the 'olde gentil Britouns' (line 57), and it is made clear from the outset that the marriage of Arveragus and Dorigen is founded upon 'gentillesse' (line 82). However, the word then disappears for hundreds of lines, only appearing once more in the final scenes. It is surprising, but what the characters have in fact done is chosen to focus on only one of the aspects of *gentillesse*: *trouthe*. As has been seen, this results in failure for all, not because *trouthe* is a bad thing, but because it should not be taken in isolation. The Middle Ages believed in the unity of the virtues, which means that all virtues are interconnected. Justice, for example, must keep company with mercy or it can result in cruelty and ultimately become unjust; honour must be tempered by generosity to others or it can result in selfishness. When the characters become motivated only by a sense of *trouthe*, they are therefore led into difficulties that can only be resolved when this virtue is placed back amongst the others. It may be true that 'Trouthe is the hyeste thing that man may kepe' (line 807) but 'highest' does not mean 'only'. It is indeed a virtue but unless it keeps company with the other virtues that make up *gentillesse* it can become a force for evil rather than good.

It is, therefore, Arveragus who saves the others, not because of his jingoistic insistence on *trouthe* but because of the act of generosity which goes with it. Sending his wife off to meet another man is, admittedly, a not unproblematic act of generosity but it does mean that Arveragus escapes from the rigid adherence to *trouthe* that has afflicted all the characters until this point, and remembers that there is more than one virtue in the world. This is the catalyst needed to make the other characters remember too. Aurelius comes face to face with 'grete gentillesse' (line 855) and is no longer willing to pursue Dorigen in the name of strict *trouthe*. He therefore releases her, claiming that he too can perform a 'gentil dede' (line 871), and indeed he has. It is as though the word has become infectious as Aurelius then uses it of the clerk, deciding that he will appeal to his *gentillesse* (line 902). The clerk declares that they have indeed behaved 'gentilly' (line 936) to one another and joins them with a 'gentil dede' (line 939) of his own as he releases Aurelius from his debt. The word that had been neglected throughout the tale comes back in abundance at the end and the characters are saved from the consequences of their own obsession with *trouthe*.

It is not the greatest example of *gentillesse* ever seen. All the characters have their faults and the concept has become a little tarnished by being left in the box so long. However, the point is that it is not an idea that should be confined to knights in shining armour. The knight gropes his way towards *gentillesse* first but, as the tale shows, the other characters are just as capable of performing *gentil* deeds of their own. It is not a concept that is intended to be limited to the high born. The message is that all ranks of society are capable of noble actions and that such virtue can be found in the streets as well as the castles. *The Franklin's Prologue and Tale* therefore moves towards a happy ending. It is a not unqualified success but without *gentillesse* it would have been a lot worse.

PACIENS

The third virtue upon which *The Franklin's Prologue and Tale* rests is patience. It is, as the Franklin declares at the beginning of the tale, a 'heigh vertu, certeyn' (line 101), high, that is, and apparently not easily attained. It is a moral quality that interests Chaucer a great deal and in his *Clerk's Tale* he presents us with patience personified in Griselda, who endures her children being taken from her and apparently killed by her husband. She even makes up the bridal bed when she is told that she is to be supplanted by a younger wife and is eventually rewarded for her great patience by being reunited with her children by a husband who had only wanted to test her endurance all along. It is an interesting story for the clerk to tell, for this kind of patience, by which the Middle Ages also meant acceptance and endurance, lies at the heart of medieval life and religion, and is advocated by the clerks, the scholars, as fundamental to the good life. Figures from the Bible such as Job were held up as an example: a man who lost his family, whose livestock died, who was beset with a plague of boils and who nevertheless remained firm in his belief in God. However, Job's patience is legendary precisely because it is exceptional and similarly, as the clerk observes at the end of his tale, it would be difficult 'nowadays to find two or three Griseldas' in the world.

Certainly, Dorigen is no Griselda. When Arveragus promises in his wedding vows that he will be patient towards his wife (line 116), it is significant that Dorigen makes no such promise in return, declaring only that no fault shall ever be found in her. It is a very worrying beginning to their marriage and the practical implications of this obvious lack of patience on Dorigen's part are made obvious when Arveragus leaves for England and she 'moorneth, waketh, waileth, fasteth, pleyneth' (line 147). It is a virtuoso performance all round but it is the 'pleyning' that is most significant. Dorigen does not just bewail Arveragus's absence to her friends, she takes her complaints to God himself, fixating on the rocks which she believes threaten her husband's safety. How can such destructive objects exist, she wants to know, in a world created by an all good and all powerful God:

> But, Lord, thise grisly feendly rokkes blake,
> That semen rather a foul confusion
> Of werk than any fair creacion
> Of swich a parfit wys God and a stable,
> Why han ye wroght this werk unresonable? (lines 196–200)

VIRTUE continued

It is a foot-stamping performance by Dorigen, culminating in the rather unequal matching of her mind against that of God, her judgement being that, 'It dooth no good, to my wit, but anoyeth' (line 203), her general annoyance still being obvious nine lines later: 'Which meenes do no good, but evere anoyen' (line 212). Clerks, she knows, have explanations (and tales of Griseldas) but she dismisses these and returns at all times to her own obsession: rocks, rocks, rocks. She does not come off well in this passionate, and slightly repetitive, complaint and it is clear that she is failing in not exhibiting any kind of patience. Indeed, her words here are familiar from one of the best-known medieval works of philosophy, Boethius's *Consolation of Philosophy*, in which a man complaining about the world is shown the error of his ways (see Background). Her lack of acceptance leads to profound doubts about God and ultimately about herself. Believing that the world really is in a state of 'foul confusion' (line 197), it is not surprising that she clutches at the apparent certainty of the courtly lady role when faced with Aurelius and ends up in the mess she does. All this because she could not show patience.

And yet, in spite of Dorigen's obvious petulance, it is difficult not to be sympathetic. The question she is asking, after all, is a great theological problem and one which has occupied the greatest philosophical minds for centuries. Dorigen knows this but dismisses the findings of the clerks, referring contemptuously to their 'argumentz' (line 214) and 'disputison' (line 218), adopting the vocabulary of medieval theological debate herself to declare that her 'conclusion' (line 217) is that all she really wants is for Arveragus to be safe. Indeed, in the face of the terrifying rocks there is something pitifully ineffectual about the disputation and arguments of the clerks. Intellectually, a medieval audience would have known that Dorigen is wrong, but at this point she seems to have a good deal of cold hard evidence on her side while God's defenders have the appearance of slick lawyers who 'wol seyn as hem leste' (line 213). Of course, this is a wrong-headed view of the universe, but it is a view that is probably familiar to many people. Further, no answer is given here. Such questioning in medieval literature is normally accompanied by an answer, the reasoning of a Lady Philosophy character or a heavenly guide who will point out that what is required is acceptance, patience, and that this need itself stems from our own lack of knowledge, not the fault of God. Such a character gives perspective to the situation but Dorigen's voice here echoes around the cliffs and there is no explicit answer to her complaint.

Of course, in spite of the fact that Dorigen's speech is couched in entirely Christian terms and is clearly dealing with a central problem of Christian theology, she is technically a pagan. This is a pagan world in which Aurelius makes his appeal to the pagan gods (to entirely no effect) and where Dorigen is to be found in the temple (line 634). The Christian answer is not available to these characters. They can, however, be virtuous pagans nevertheless. Patience, suffering and endurance are still open to them in spite of the fact that they are not explicitly offered as the solution to their problems by a convenient Christian moral guide. Once again, it is Arveragus who sets the process in motion. Confronted with Dorigen's hasty promise, he responds with the dogged endurance that he had promised his wife in the beginning:

> 'Ye, wyf,' quod he, 'lat slepen that is stille.
> It may be wel, paraventure, yet to day' (lines 800–1)

It is in many ways a horrible response, but patience is perhaps the most difficult of all the virtues to sell to anyone. Certainly, the clerk does not manage it with his Griselda, the likelihood of finding two or three women of such patience in the world being considerably reduced by the time they have heard his tale of noble suffering. Active virtues are always more attractive than passive endurance in the face of misery and Arveragus's patient platitudes and tears do nothing for the virtue's overall reputation. Nevertheless, it is ultimately what saves all the characters. In their non-Christian way they speak of *gentillesse* and this is a reasonable catch-all term for their behaviour in the closing stages of the tale. The catalyst remains, however, a profoundly Christian virtue. All the characters ultimately face their suffering: Arveragus will endure the torment of his wife being dispatched to another man; Dorigen is sent to suffer whether she likes it or not; Aurelius learns to endure the torment of a life without Dorigen's love and accepts that he may have to suffer the indignity of life 'a-begged' in his 'kirtle bare' (line 908); and the clerk tolerantly accepts that his efforts will go without payment.

Thus, *The Franklin's Prologue and Tale* engages with three important moral concepts: the feudal notion of *trouthe*; the courtly morality of *gentillesse*; and the Christian idea of patient endurance.

Trouthe is discovered to be useless, if not to say harmful, when isolated from other virtues and so the characters seize upon the much broader *gentillesse* to save themselves in the end. Even this, however, is not enough, for sending Dorigen to Aurelius would be ridiculous as an act of gentility. The catalyst is instead the far more deeply Christian virtue of patience. The Franklin's words at the beginning of the tale are relevant to the end:

> Lerneth to suffre, or elles, so moot I goon,
> Ye shul it lerne, wher so ye wole or noon. (lines 105–6)

'Suffer' is exactly what our characters have learned to do by the end of the tale but such a moral cannot make for a truly happy ending. Dorigen and Arveragus are parcelled up, labelled as 'blissful' and dismissed by the Franklin who refuses to talk about them any more. Aurelius too is curiously tight-lipped, finishing his own story with words that echo the Franklin: 'ther is namoore to seyn' (line 934). Meanwhile the clerk dismisses the debt with a **simile** that leaves us with a curious image of Aurelius as first cousin to a worm:

> Sire, I releesse the thy thousand pound,
> As thou right now were cropen out of the ground (lines 941–2)

Without a Christian framework in which to place their suffering, how to suffer is, in fact, all they do learn.

SETTING

The setting throughout *The Franklin's Prologue and Tale* is very important. Normally, **romances** take place in uniformly courtly landscapes: castles and great houses with a few dangerous forests and woods inhabited by monsters. The Franklin begins his tale this way, setting it in the romantic and distant sounding 'Armorik' (line 57) and giving Dorigen a 'castel faste by the see' (line 175) to live in. It is a good courtly beginning but both the castle and Armorica have disappeared by the end of the tale. Even in the very first line, the Franklin cannot resist explaining to us that 'Armorik' is really Brittany, thus removing his Romance from never-never land and setting it in the real world. Indeed, he goes even further than this, telling us that Arveragus and Dorigen lived, 'Nat far fro Pedmark' (line 129), a place on the Breton cape. The place had made the news in the late fourteenth century as the scene of various ship-seizing incidents involving the English. It was not, therefore, a fanciful name but a real place familiar to an English audience. And, as if this were not enough, we even get to hear that Arveragus himself came from another village, a place Chaucer calls 'Kayrrud' (line 136), probably modern Kerru. The place-names and detailed description of the coastline mean that it is almost possible to identify the very spot at which Dorigen makes her lament about the rocks. All of this is highly unusual for a romance, where the knight normally travels in a highly stylised and completely unidentifiable landscape. However, as has been seen throughout, this is a tale that questions **stereotypes** and conventions.

The next shift in scene takes us to a May garden, familiar once more from medieval romance, but even here the description is not as traditional as it might have been (see Extended Commentaries, Text 2). Even the 'magician' is not firmly placed in the land of fantasy. The two brothers encounter him specifically 'two furlong or thre' (line 500) from the university town of Orleans and any expectations of caves or underground vaults are swept aside by the firm assertion that our magician is a clerk who lives in a 'hous' (line 515), and a very comfortable house at that. Magic is performed in the 'studie' (line 542) and is again geographically specific: the rocks are to be removed from Brittany, 'And eek from Gerounde to the mouth of Sayne' (line 550). It should come as no surprise, therefore, when Aurelius finally encounters Dorigen not in some romantic garden but in a medieval main street. The narrator has apparently even forgotten that she ever lived in a clifftop castle and has Aurelius watching her 'hous' (line 835) and running to encounter her 'right in the quikkest strete' (line 830).

This is not the idealistic landscape of medieval romance, for it is not the idealistic world that romance presents either. A knight, a lady and a squire may be the stock characters of such a world, and they do act, particularly in the beginning, as though they were really damsels in towers or the heroes of courtly poetry. However, their beliefs and actions have been taken out of the romance world and placed in the real world where marriages, relationships and oaths face problems that cannot be dealt with by a sharp sword. This is why the landscape is so specific and changes in the course of the tale as the characters have to face their difficulties.

STRUCTURE

The plot of *The Franklin's Tale* is, by its very nature, symmetrical: a woman makes a rash promise and it must be fulfilled. However, Cooper (1989) has pointed out that there is even greater symmetry in the tale than this. In fact, the story falls into two halves that mirror each other. This is best seen in a diagram that follows the plot down the left-hand column and up the right:

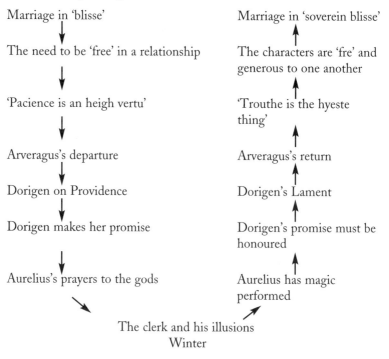

It is clear from this diagram that illusion lies at the very centre of the tale. From the moment that Aurelius prays to Apollo to upset the natural order of things until the clerk performs his magic, illusion dominates. This is the darkest point of the tale, literally, as we have also reached midwinter. However, it is a winter that also contains hope as the god with two faces, Janus, is present. He appears at the centre of the tale and looks both ways. There is, after all, a chance of a happy outcome. Such a structure also implies that it may be more than a 'chance'. Dorigen makes her complaint against irrational Fortune (line 683), and against Providence (lines 193–221), and laments at all times that there is chaos all around her. However, the tale proves that there is indeed order in the universe, a message that is borne out by the structure of the tale itself (see Sources, Boethius).

LANGUAGE & STYLE

THE FRANKLIN AS NARRATOR

The Franklin begins his tale by declaring that he is a *burel* ('unlearned') man and asks the company to excuse his rough speech. It is the medieval equivalent of beginning a speech with the words, 'unaccustomed as I am to public speaking', and is used mostly by those who do not think they are unaccustomed to it at all. It is, in fact, a **rhetorical** device. Rhetoric, the art of public speaking, was treated very seriously in the Middle Ages and the Franklin, far from being the plain-talking man he claims to be, is a devotee of its use. His whole prologue, in which he says he knows nothing about rhetoric, is really highly rhetorical: a modesty device known as *diminutio*.

Playing on the word 'colours', a technical term for rhetorical ornamentation, the Franklin declares that the only colours he knows about are those found in paint boxes, dyes or the pretty hues of a field: 'Colours of rethoryk been to me queynte' (line 54), he says. But the very fact that he knows the technical terminology is significant, and the wordplay itself is another rhetorical device. He claims to be unlearned but skips through classical references, even giving the ancient author Cicero his full name (line 50), something not done elsewhere in Chaucer. In fact, this 'plain man' presents us with one of the most elaborately rhetorical of all *The Canterbury Tales* and rivals any other pilgrim in classical name-dropping. There are also many old-fashioned terms in *The Franklin's*

Tale, which are not used anywhere else in Chaucer's writing, words such as *sursanure* (line 441) for a wound healed only on the surface, or *serement* (line 862) for a legal contract. And why use the name Brittany, the Franklin seems to think, when he can use its archaic form, *Armorica* (line 57), instead? Only, it is not 'instead'. The Franklin has to stop and explain that what he really means is Brittany, and this is a feature of the whole tale. It is not an effortless display of learning and rhetoric but a very self-conscious attempt by a man with some pretensions to tell a grand story. Sometimes he is successful, and there are many beautiful and skilful passages in the tale. At other times, however, the whole thing comes crashing down around his ears. It is one thing to say that, 'th'orisonte hath reft the sonne his light' but to follow it with the explanation, 'This is as muche to seye as it was night' (lines 345–6) merely undermines the Franklin's rhetorical skill and reveals the plain-speaking man within. He cannot resist interrupting the flow of his story to give a formal description of the garden (lines 901–17), or an elegant piece on December (lines 572–83), not to mention the twenty-two classical legends referred to by Dorigen in her marathon complaint (lines 750–84), but enthusiastic excess is part of the Franklin's character.

The exuberant, well-meaning, but slightly pretentious Franklin is not, then, without his faults as a narrator. His boundless enthusiasm for a courtly world outside his own experience means that the rhetorical devices can be piled on too thickly, and the classical references can come a bit too thick and fast on occasion. His language can also become convoluted, or simply difficult to translate, as he wrestles with concepts that he finds difficult to explain, but this, at least, may not be entirely his fault. Ultimately, the Franklin is trying to present an alternative way of living, an ideal world in which men and women are equals and live lives of nobility and perfect virtue. If the Franklin's language is not always adequate to describe this world of mutual bliss it may be because, until this point, there has been no need for such language.

IMAGERY & SYMBOLISM

The **romance** setting may be undermined in the course of *The Franklin's Tale* but it is still, especially in the opening stages, very much a **symbolic** landscape. The black rocks of Brittany are one of the most pervasive images in the tale as they come to dominate not just the coastline but every waking thought of Dorigen. They are symbolic in her own mind of the dangers and hostility of a world that seems to her not just threatening but downright chaotic. Gazing down from the clifftops she sees 'many a ship and barge' (line 178) and fears for their safety among the 'grisly rokkes blake' (line 187). Only a few lines further on, they become the 'grisly *feendly* rokkes blake' (line 196), an interesting addition as hell was traditionally viewed in the Middle Ages as a barren and rocky place. She stands at the very 'brinke' of the cliffs (line 186) and stares down into the depths. It is a hellish description and Dorigen's terror is directed towards the fate of the little boats making their way to a safe harbour. The Middle Ages often presented the soul as just such a little boat, tossed around on the sea of life, attempting to avoid coming to grief on the rocks of sin, and hoping at last to reach the safety of the port of heaven. In her tirade against the rocks, therefore, Dorigen is doing more than simply worrying about Arveragus, she is questioning the existence of evil in the world, wondering how it is that God could allow any of his creatures to suffer 'stormy' lives and be lost on the 'rocks' of sin.

Staring literally down into the void causes Dorigen to experience near vertigo and to collapse dizzily onto the ground. This dizziness is in itself symbolic, suggesting that Dorigen is not being remotely clear-headed as she questions God's ability to control the universe. Indeed, in spite of the existence of the rocks, the description of the boats shows them calmly 'Seillinge hir cours, where as hem liste go' (line 179). Rocks or no rocks, whether evil exists in the universe or not, the little boats can sail happily through, at least if that is what they want or *liste* to do. People have free will, to choose sin or avoid it, but what Dorigen wants to do is refuse to accept the existence of evil and this is a far more dangerous course of action than understanding why the rocks are there and learning how to avoid them. This is the great danger in the tale and not the rocks themselves. Put simply, the rocks symbolise evil for Dorigen but they become in turn symbolic of her own unyielding personality (see Characterisation, on Dorigen) as she fails to understand their place in the universe.

What Dorigen does not realise is that she is safe and protected in her solid stone castle (line 175) on the cliffs. This is God's landscape and if she were to accept this world patiently then Arveragus would return to her and she would not have to greet him with tears and her tale of woe. The real danger occurs when man attempts to 'improve' upon the world and upon the divine plan. Thus, Dorigen is safe amongst the rocks but right 'ther biside' (line 230) is a garden, created with the 'craft of mannes hand' (line 237) and it is here in this soft green landscape of flowers and plants that Dorigen is truly threatened (see Extended Commentaries, Text 2). The boats and the cliff-top castle may be associated with danger in the mind of Dorigen but there is no harm done here. However, the same images occur later in the text when the brother of Aurelius is thinking of ways in which to trap Dorigen and force her to keep her promise. He remembers seeing conjurors perform who,

> ... withinne an halle large,
> Have maad come in a water and a barge,
> And in the halle rowen up and doun ...
> Somtime a castel, al of lym and stoon;
> And whan hem liked, voided it anon. (lines 471–8)

There is a great difference between the little 'barge' of Dorigen's early complaint which went sailing wherever it liked, and this 'barge' of man's illusions which is compelled to row pointlessly up and down. Similarly, the mighty stone castle is easily 'voided' by the conjuror, a word that implies more emptiness than simply being made to disappear. There is nothing wrong with God's plan for the universe: it is the man-made world that is small-minded, pointless and ultimately truly threatening. This is what Dorigen, and even Aurelius, finally learn.

Only once Dorigen has made her bargain with Aurelius and faces the consequences of the rocks being removed does she understand that they are not intrinsically evil but rather that their obliteration is 'agains the proces of nature' (line 673). Indeed, the opening section of Dorigen's catalogue of suicides, before she descends into irrelevance and bathos, offers some moving examples of women who showed both great courage and a great fondness for the rocks and immersing waters that had been the stuff of Dorigen's earlier nightmares. Rocks were not the problem for the daughters of King Phidon, rather they were forced to writhe and dance naked on a man-made stone 'pavement' (line 702) which was covered with their father's blood. Faced with the choice of death or further torment they preferred to drown themselves. As for the fifty virgins of Sparta, they danced to the cliffs and threw themselves onto the rocks below rather than be raped and tortured by the invading men of Messene (lines 707–13). The catalogue gets out of hand but not before it provides many tales of the horrors that men can perpetrate both on women and on one another. Finally, as Dorigen comes to realise, the rocks are not a symbol of evil, such evil is man-made, rather they are a sign that there is order in the universe and that the real danger is in failing to realise this.

PART FOUR

EXTENDED COMMENTARIES

TEXT 1 (LINES 89–126)

For o thing, sires, saufly dar I seye,
That freendes everich oother moot obeye,   90
If they wol longe holden compaignye.
Love wol nat been constreyned by maistrye.
Whan maistrie comth, the God of Love anon
Beteth his winges, and farewel, he is gon!
Love is a thing as any spirit free.   95
Wommen, of kinde, desiren libertee,
And nat to been constreyned as a thral;
And so doon men, if I sooth seyen shal.
Looke who that is moost pacient in love,
He is at his avantage al above.   100
Pacience is an heigh vertu, certeyn,
For it venquisseth, as thise clerkes seyn,
Thinges that rigour sholde nevere atteyne.
For every word men may nat chide or pleyne.
Lerneth to suffre, or elles, so moot I goon,   105
Ye shul it lerne, wher so ye wole or noon;
For in this world, certein, ther no wight is
That he ne dooth or seith somtime amis.
Ire, siknesse, or constellacioun,
Wyn, wo, or chaunginge of complexioun   110
Causeth ful ofte to doon amis or speken.
On every wrong a man may nat be wreken.
After the time moste be temperaunce
To every wight that kan on governaunce.
And therfore hath this wise, worthy knight,   115
To live in ese, suffrance hire bihight,
And she to him ful wisly gan to swere
That nevere sholde ther be defaute in here.

> Heere may men seen an humble, wys accord;
> Thus hath she take hir servant and hir lord –   120
> Servant in love, and lord in mariage.
> Thanne was he bothe in lordshipe and servage.
> Servage? nay, but in lordshipe above,
> Sith he hath bothe his lady and his love;
> His lady, certes, and his wyf also,   125
> The which that lawe of love acordeth to.

The Franklin has only just begun his tale when he interrupts the flow of his own narrative to give his views on marriage. It is a piece of 'wisdom' and while it is common, and recommended in works on **rhetoric**, to begin a story with a wise saying known as a *sententia*, the whole story is not supposed to be so blatantly interrupted once it is under way. It is also on the long side, but it is typical of the Franklin who does not fade into the background once his tale begins but rather intrudes on the narrative from time to time in order to comment on the behaviour of his characters (e.g. lines 412–14). In spite of his protestations that he is a 'burel man' (line 44) he has a fondness for rhetoric and indulges it at many points in the tale, both in his own speech and in the speech of Aurelius and, particularly, Dorigen. What begins here as an intimate address to the audience, apparently offering to take them into his confidence about his own personal thoughts, will become a grand declaration about the nature of marriage, becoming increasingly more rhetorical until it collapses under its own weight.

It does, however, begin plainly and positively enough. The aim is to look at the desires of both men and women, and the Franklin states that their desires are the same. Women are even mentioned first (line 96) in a way that implies that they are not second-class citizens, and there is a general spirit of reciprocity:

> … freendes everich oother moot obeye
> If they wol longe holden compaignye (lines 90–1)

It seems like a positive start but this is the last time that the plural pronoun is used in the passage. Once the Franklin has mentioned men in the tenth line everything thereafter becomes male centred and singular and the promising mutuality of 'they' disappears. 'He' and 'men' are used insistently and while women are implicitly included in these terms, they are explicitly excluded. This world of ideal marriage turns out to be a man's world, full of male 'clerkes' (line 102), addressed to 'sires' (line 89), where even Venus has been replaced by her son as 'God of Love' (lines 93–4). It is not a promising environment in which to attempt to talk of women as equals and of a love based on agreement.

The Franklin's message, as he sees it, is that, 'Love is a thing as any spirit free' (line 95). 'Free' is an important word in the tale with its dual meaning of liberty and generosity. It is the part of *gentillesse* that will save the characters from their terrible fates in the end and is an essential part, as the Franklin rightly points out, of all good relations. In spite of this, 'free' and 'libertee' (line 96) are mentioned only once each, stuck together in a nice little couplet and entirely isolated from the rest of the passage. Words for constraint and dominance, on the other hand, abound: 'obeye', 'maistrye', 'constreyned', 'thral', 'venquisseth', 'servage' etc. The tone of the passage is completely at odds with what it claims to be saying. Freedom in love may well be the intended message but the overall impression is of a world that cannot escape from bondage.

It is not even clear that this love is worth saving. It is personified as Cupid, traditionally armed to the teeth with arrows, striking out blindly to wound those in his path. The destructive force of Cupid's kind of love is seen later in the tale as Aurelius is tormented by his 'sursanure' (line 441), the wound which heals on the surface but festers fatally underneath. To this bleak image is added, 'Ire, siknesse, … constellacioun, / Wyn, wo, … chaunginge of complexioun' (lines 109–16). In the midst of these images of suffering the only advice the Franklin can give is:

> Lerneth to suffre, or elles, so moot I goon,
> Ye shul it lerne, wher so ye wole or noon (lines 105–6)

It sounds, in fact, more like a threat than well-intentioned advice. The message, of course, is that patience is necessary in all human relationships, and the suffering meant is really only 'toleration'. However, we have seen too much bleakness here not to be reminded of the other definition of the word.

Certainly, when Arveragus pledges 'suffrance' (line 116) to his wife, her response indicates that he will have to suffer in both senses of the word. The Franklin's view of marriage has been grim but sensible as he points out that everyone makes mistakes. To this Dorigen cheerfully swears, 'That nevere sholde ther be defaute in here' (line 118). In so doing she effectively dismisses the two main points of the Franklin's argument: the need for patience with one another's faults, and the necessity of freedom.

This declaration is what effectively propels the Franklin into a rhetorical extravaganza. His fantasy of a marriage based on equality was already on very shaky ground, but there was at least some common sense in what he had to say. Following Dorigen's vow, however, he attempts to clarify exactly what he means and in the process becomes increasingly confused. The language of **courtly love** provides him with the word 'servant' for a woman's lover, while the language of matrimony provides him with the word 'lord'. The Franklin therefore attempts to juggle the terms to come up with a way of describing this new relationship:

> Thus hath she take hir servant and hir lord –
> Servant in love, and lord in mariage.
> Thanne was he bothe in lordshipe and servage.
> Servage? nay, but in lordshipe above (lines 120–3)

The words are tossed to and fro but the Franklin does not get any further forward. For that he would need a new vocabulary but such a thing is not available to him. He is attempting to create a new world but the terms at his disposal are as inflexible as Dorigen's rocks. It is not his fault. Even Dorigen has settled into the old way of life before he has even finished explaining the new one. He therefore stumbles on, covering his confusion with increasing rhetorical flourishes: a quick *contentio* (**paradox** – lines 120–1) followed by *interrogatio* (rhetorical question – line 123), followed swiftly by *correctio* (substituting a more suitable expression – lines 123–4). His verbal acrobatics, however, come crashing down in the final line as he speaks of the 'lawe' (line 126) of love. All his talk of freedom has merely brought us back to the traditional constraining image.

TEXT 2   (LINES 223–256)

> Hire freendes sawe that it was no disport
> To romen by the see, but disconfort,
> And shopen for to pleyen somwher elles.   225

They leden hire by riveres and by welles,
And eek in othere places delitables;
They dauncen and they pleyen at ches and tables.
    So on a day, right in the morwe-tide,
Unto a gardyn that was ther biside,   230
In which that they hadde maad hir ordinaunce
Of vitaille and of oother purveiaunce,
They goon and pleye hem al the longe day.
And this was on the sixte morwe of May,
Which May hadde peynted with his softe shoures   235
This gardyn ful of leves and of floures;
And craft of mannes hand so curiously
Arrayed hadde this gardyn trewely,
That nevere was ther gardyn of swich prys
But if it were the verray paradis.   240
The odour of floures and the fresshe sighte
Wolde han maked any herte lighte
That evere was born, but if to greet siknesse
Or to greet sorwe, helde it in distresse,
So ful it was of beautee with plesaunce.   245
At after-diner gonne they to daunce,
And singe also, save Dorigen allone,
Which made alwey hir compleint and hir moone,
For she ne saugh him on the daunce go
That was hir housbonde and hir love also.   250
But natheless she moste a time abide
And with good hope lete hir sorwe slide.
    Upon this daunce, amonges othere men,
Daunced a squier biforn Dorigen,
That fressher was and jolier of array,   255
As to my doom, than is the month of May.

Landscape is important throughout *The Franklin's Prologue and Tale* (see Setting) and this passage uses a garden setting to undermine the **courtly love** tradition of which it is normally a crucial part. The May garden is traditionally the home of courtly love, the place where its rules are kept and where those who adhere to those rules flourish. However, there is something unsettling about this garden, and something worrying about those who 'pleyen' in it. The idea of 'play', first of all, is a little too insistent. The word is repeated three times in the space of nine lines as Dorigen and her friends decide to go and 'pleyen' (line 225) together, 'pleyen at ches and tables' (line 228), and, in fact, 'pleye hem al the longe day' (line 233). The people who had roamed aimlessly by the sea are now engaged in games that are just as purposeless. There is an emphasis upon pleasure that is worrying in a medieval context. Games are acceptable in their place but not to the level of excess presented here.

The artificial nature of games is mirrored in the artificiality of the garden itself. Its beauty looks as though it has been 'peynted' (line 235) and it is made clear that it is not the unenhanced product of nature, but has been created by 'craft of mannes hand' (line 237). It is, in fact, a highly contrived landscape and as such is a wholly suitable setting for the scene of courtly love that is about to follow, as Aurelius declares his love to Dorigen for the first time. There is nothing 'natural' about this form of love. It is bound round with codes and rules and is as artificial as the garden itself. The lady may be said to have all the power but she is merely like the queen in the game of chess they play (line 228): she has power for the duration of the game but no longer. Real power belongs to the men and it is worth noting that even May is male here (line 235). This is Aurelius's world:

> That fressher was and jolier of array,
>
> As to my doom, than is the month of May. (lines 255–6)

Dorigen, on the other hand, is a solitary figure whose only movement in the passage is to be passively led by her friends (line 226).

The beauty of the place is reminiscent of Paradise (line 240) but this too is problematic. The last time there was a man and a woman together in a 'paradisal' garden the whole of humanity found themselves cast into a cold, hard world of death and destruction. The Middle Ages knew its Bible and would be reminded of Adam and Eve in the Garden of Eden. On the surface all is well but in the very act of trying to assure us of its beauty, the narrator introduces another worrying element. Anyone would have been made happy by it, he says, unless great sickness,

> Or to greet sorwe helde it in distresse,
>
> So ful it was of beautee with plesaunce (lines 244–5)

Text 2 continued

Distress and pleasure are suddenly side by side. It is a typical Chaucerian device, to introduce doubts in the very act of allegedly doing the opposite. There is now sickness, sorrow and distress in our Garden of Love. The initial impression of pretty May flowers and springtime joy has been undermined.

Unusually for a romance, Chaucer even tells us the date. This is a technique that he uses throughout the tale. The setting is specific, we are aware of the seasons changing, the time and the date. It is, we are told, 6 May (line 234). In courtly love literature, the lovers are not constrained by time. Their love exists in an eternal spring untouched by the outside world. Chaucer denies it this privilege here. Courtly love is being forced out into the real world and is being exposed for the constraining, artificial game it really is. To prove the point, Chaucer even draws attention to the passing of time while his characters are in the garden, placing them there in the morning (line 229) and noting that their dancing takes place, 'after-diner' (line 246). As for the date itself, it seems likely that it has some extra significance. It is included in medieval lists of 'inauspicious days' and, while not the unluckiest day in the month, it was certainly a day of potential trouble. It is yet another detail that adds to the sinister feel of a garden that is superficially a place of joy and love.

The reference to 'after-diner' is also worth noting. It may be a reflection of the well-fed Franklin's interests, but characters in this tale are always very concerned where their next meal is coming from. The clerk is much occupied with thoughts of his supper (line 517), and even our Garden of Love is occupied by people whose first concern is for their stomachs. The first thing they do is organise their 'vitaille and ... oother purveiaunce' (line 232). Courtly love collides head-on with reality once more. It is a brief description but it alerts us to a number of Chaucer's key ideas in this tale. Courtly love is just a game, and a problematic game at that. He will, therefore, drag it and all its conventions out into the day-to-day world and see what happens.

TEXT 3   (LINES 639–73)

'My righte lady,' quod this woful man,
'Whom I moost drede and love as I best kan,   640

And lothest were of al this world displese,
Nere it that I for yow have swich disese
That I moste dien heere at youre foot anon,
Noght wolde I telle how me is wo bigon.
But certes outher moste I die or pleyne;   645
Ye sle me giltelees for verray peyne.
But of my deeth thogh that ye have no routhe,
Aviseth yow er that ye breke youre trouthe.
Repenteth yow, for thilke God above,
Er ye me sleen by cause that I yow love.   650
For, madame, wel ye woot what ye han hight –
Nat that I chalange any thing of right
Of yow, my soverein lady, but youre grace –
But in a gardyn yond, at swich a place,
Ye woot right wel what ye bihighten me;   655
And in myn hand youre trouthe plighten ye
To love me best – God woot, ye seyde so,
Al be that I unworthy am therto.
Madame, I speke it for the honour of yow
Moore than to save myn hertes lyf right now,   –   660
I have do so as ye comanded me;
And if ye vouche sauf, ye may go see.
Dooth as yow list; have youre biheste in minde,
For, quik or deed, right there ye shal me finde.
In yow lith al to do me live or deye –   665
But wel I woot the rokkes been aweye.'
    He taketh his leve, and she astoned stood;
In al hir face nas a drope of blood.
She wende nevere han come in swich a trappe.
'Allas,' quod she, 'that evere this sholde happe!   670
For wende I nevere by possibilitee
That swich a monstre or merveille mighte be!
It is agains the proces of nature.'

Courtly love plays an important part in *The Franklin's Tale*: we first see
Dorigen as a courtly lady and this is how Aurelius behaves towards her
until the very end of the tale, seeing himself throughout as the tormented

servant of love. His performance reaches its peak in this passage as he seeks out Dorigen to tell her that he has accomplished the task she set him. All the traditional **imagery** and language of courtly love are found here, for Aurelius is faithful to everything he has ever read about this lover's code. Rule One is that the lover should be in constant fear of losing his mistress, of not being worthy of her, or of displeasing her in any way. Aurelius therefore approaches Dorigen in a state of 'drede' (line 640), telling her that he would be 'lothest … [to] displese' (line 641) her of all the people in the world. Rule Two is that the lover should always be in a position of inferiority and Aurelius accordingly declares himself to be 'unworthy' (line 658), begging his lady for mercy, and telling her that his life is in her hands. Rule Three is that the lover should strive to be more worthy by performing deeds of chivalry and fulfilling every task his lady sets him. Accordingly, Aurelius is now before Dorigen. It takes him thirty-eight meandering lines to get to the point, but the rocks are gone!

It is a thoroughly unappealing performance. With his usual excess, Aurelius declares that he is on the point of death no less than eight times, making his customary offer even to die at Dorigen's feet in his very first sentence (line 643, cf. line 304). 'Outher moste I die or pleyne' (line 645) he declares, but chooses, as always, to avail himself of the complaining option. The reader becomes conscious that this is nothing more than a façade: Dorigen is not the stern and powerful lady of courtly love literature; Aurelius does not live in fear of her frown; and he is not, unsurprisingly, about to die of love. Instead, all the power is in his hands. There are almost as many 'promise' references here as references to his impending death. The speech may be masquerading as the humble offering of the lady's servant in love but the reality is very different.

Aurelius proceeds with an almost legalistic attitude towards Dorigen's 'trouthe' (line 648). He claims to be a courtly lover but the task she sets him is not treated like a courtly task that will allow him to become an even nobler man. It is treated like a legal contract and Aurelius is asserting his 'rights' under the guise of begging for 'mercy':

> Nat that I chalange any thing of right
> Of yow, my soverein lady, but youre grace – (lines 652–3)

It is entirely illogical: 'grace', mercy, is one thing that cannot be demanded as a right. Aurelius is adopting the stance of humble servant but is in fact making demands on Dorigen. Even in the very act of telling her that she is free to do as she chooses he is reminding her that she is not free in his eyes: 'Dooth as yow list; have youre biheste in minde' (line 663). She is hemmed in at every turn. It is blackmail and coercion under the guise of courtliness and concern and Aurelius does not stop short of telling an outright lie:

> Madame, I speke it for the honour of yow
> Moore than to save myn hertes lyf right now, – (lines 659–60)

He is not thinking of Dorigen, he is thinking of himself and even if he were not, Dorigen's honour is not at stake here. Only a single-minded, litigious approach to *trouthe* would divorce it from the other aspects of *gentillesse*.

What begins, therefore, as a courtly address to a powerful lady is revealed to be a slimy performance that in fact denies the lady any power at all. This is the reality behind the romantic façade of courtly love. It is a beautiful sounding literary device but the man will not in reality be content to die at his lady's feet, consoled only by a smile. Aurelius harks back to the garden of their first encounter (lines 654–5), a place of artifice and illusion where the language of courtly love was more in keeping with the surroundings. Now, however, he and Dorigen are in the local temple, a less romantic environment in which we can begin to see the courtly façade crack. Dorigen is not the haughty lady of the stories, she is reduced to the level of an animal as she is caught in a 'trappe' (line 669). This is where Aurelius wants her to be, not on a pedestal where she cannot be reached.

The setting for this interview is also interesting from the point of view of Dorigen's theology. Ancient literature states that, 'when the gods wish to punish us they answer our prayers'. Standing in her temple, Dorigen discovers that her prayer has been answered and suffers more than she ever did before. Earlier, when she had questioned God, she had declared the world to be 'a foul confusion' (line 197). She could not comprehend how the rocks could fit into any reasonable plan for the universe and had condemned the world as chaotic. Now, however, she realises that it is the removal of the rocks which is 'agains the proces of nature' (line 673) and not their existence. Aurelius's act is therefore an unnatural one, a 'monstre' (line 672). Indeed, it is a petrifying monster that leaves Dorigen 'astoned' (line 667). There is order in the universe, though Dorigen comes to the knowledge a little too late. Both she and Aurelius strive against nature, Dorigen in wanting to pick and choose the parts that she believes should be there, because she cannot see the overall picture. It is **ironic**, therefore, that Aurelius tells her she 'may go see' (line 662) that the rocks are gone, for 'seeing' is not Dorigen's strong point. She never does go to see what he has done, but the real danger of the rocks was always in her own head so she need not travel far. The rocks, which had not posed much of a threat in God's world, are now a major threat in the world that Dorigen and Aurelius have created between them.

PART FIVE

BACKGROUND

GEOFFREY CHAUCER'S LIFE & WORK

Geoffrey Chaucer was born in London in the early 1340s, most probably in 1343, the son, possibly the only son, of John Chaucer and his wife Agnes. The family originated in Ipswich where they had been called de Dynyngton or le Taverner and it seems likely that Geoffrey Chaucer's great grandfather had been a tavern keeper. Geoffrey's grandfather, Robert de Dynyngton, appears to have worked for a merchant but when the merchant died in a brawl in 1302, Robert inherited some of his property. The family was now far more prosperous and as a result of this change in fortune they also changed their name. They took the name of their dead benefactor: Chaucer.

They settled in London where John Chaucer, Geoffrey's father, became a very prosperous wine merchant. He supplied wine to the king's cellars, supervising imports from France. He was influential and successful and was heavily involved in the business and political affairs of the city. His wealth and connections meant that he could provide his young son with many advantages, beginning with Geoffrey's enrolment as a page in the royal household.

A page was a boy between the ages of ten and seventeen who was an attendant in the house of a noble family. Effectively he was a servant but in this way a boy could learn about polite society and hopefully be accepted by a patron, someone who would take an interest in him and help his career. The young Geoffrey became a page to the Countess of Ulster, the king's daughter-in-law, and eventually served her husband, Prince Lionel.

It was in the service of Prince Lionel that Geoffrey was captured in France. Edward III made an unsuccessful attempt to gain the French throne in 1359 and Geoffrey Chaucer is named among those for whom a ransom was paid. After this, he seems to have entered the direct service of the king, though his diplomatic skills seem to have been more in demand than his military expertise. He was sent on diplomatic missions to Spain, France and Italy over the next few years and some of the business appears to have been of a very secret nature.

Chaucer's social standing was also improved by his marriage in 1365 to Philippa Pan (or de Roet), a lady in the household of Queen Philippa, Edward III's wife. Philippa's sister Katherine was the mistress, and eventually third wife, of John of Gaunt, the rich and powerful son of Edward III. Chaucer's marriage to Philippa therefore connected him more intimately to the rich and powerful circle of John of Gaunt and the royal court. John's son by his first marriage would later become King Henry IV and Chaucer's nephews were therefore half-brothers to the future king.

However, Chaucer's daily life does not seem to have been drastically altered by his family connections. In fact, in 1374 he was appointed to a new position with the customs department in London, a move that took him away from the court. He was responsible for checking the quantities of wool, sheepskins and hides being shipped abroad so that the correct export duty could be charged. He was still sent overseas on state business and these trips probably brought him into contact with the works of the great European poets.

In 1389 he was appointed to a new position: clerk of the king's works. Still a civil servant, his new post meant that he was in charge of overseeing the building and repair of the king's properties. He supervised the workmen, paid the wages and saw that the plans were properly implemented. However, paying the wages proved to be more of a problem than it sounds. Chaucer was robbed, certainly once but possibly three times in the space of four days, as he attempted to deliver the money. It may have been a relief, therefore, when he was instructed to give up the post a few months later.

Chaucer now retired from the king's service but he continued to receive annual payments from the court, together with gifts such as a fur-trimmed, scarlet gown from the future Henry IV and an annual tun (252 gallons) of wine from Richard II. An occasional poem on the state of his purse ensured that his pension arrived on time but most of his creative energy was focused on one work, *The Canterbury Tales*. This was the last decade of Chaucer's life. He died on 25 October 1400, *The Canterbury Tales* unfinished. He was buried in one of the more humble chapels in Westminster Abbey but his body was later moved to the east aisle of the south transept, where he became the first tenant of 'Poet's Corner'.

His OTHER WORKS

The earliest work we have by Chaucer is the *Romaunt of the Rose*, a liberal translation of part of a famous French work. It is an exploration of the nature of love including everything from sex and friendship to love of God. Many of the themes of this text, including **courtly love**, were later to be explored again by Chaucer in *The Franklin's Prologue and Tale*.

Chaucer's next major work was probably *The Book of the Duchess*, a poem of consolation for John of Gaunt following the death of his first wife, Blanche, in 1368. *The Parlement of Foules* (*c*.1368) is also probably linked to an historical event. In this poem a dreamer watches as the birds gather to choose their mates on St Valentine's Day. The complicated nature of love is seen in the eagle who must choose between her three suitors, possibly a reference to the much-courted Anne of Bohemia who finally married Richard II on 3 May 1381.

Love becomes even more complicated and far less successful in Chaucer's next poem, the great *Troilus and Criseyde*. Here Chaucer tells us the story of Prince Troilus who loved Criseyde and how she betrayed him before she died. However, in his next poem, Chaucer declares that he will make amends to women. In *The Legend of Good Women* he tells how the God of Love chastised him for telling the story of Criseyde and for translating his *Romaunt of the Rose* and he promises (we assume not wholly seriously) to tell only good stories about women in future. He worked for a few years on this project but never finished it, turning his attention instead to *The Canterbury Tales* around 1387.

Like *The Legend of Good Women*, *The Canterbury Tales* is a collection of individual stories but the tone and setting are very different. This is not presented as a dream populated by gods and goddesses but is instead a tale of ordinary people set in the real world of the fourteenth century. There is a knight in the company and some of the group (the Franklin included) do tell stories about knights and ladies, but Chaucer is no longer concerned only with the court. Merchants, millers, ploughmen and sailors are all the object of his attention. The issues that had concerned him in his earlier poetry are still found here but are given wider application. Almost all medieval society rides up to tell a tale and these are as likely to be humorous and obscene as courtly and tragic.

HISTORICAL BACKGROUND

One day in October 1347, a boat arrived in the port of Messina in Sicily. When the hatches were opened the boat was found to be full of dead and dying men, their bodies swollen and blackened by some terrible disease. The bubonic plague, the Black Death, had arrived in Europe. It spread quickly, carried by black rats that nested on board ships, and was transmitted to humans through fleabites. By 1349 the disease had taken hold in England and within the year around a third of the population (1.5 million) were dead.

The deaths of so many people inevitably had a powerful effect on medieval life. The traditional picture of the Middle Ages was of the church and the aristocracy, both small but powerful groups, being supported by the labour of vast numbers of peasants. This system had already begun to break down by the time Chaucer was born but it had not gone completely. The arrival of the plague, or 'the death' as it was known in the Middle Ages, changed this. For the first time, peasant labour was in short supply. Peasants could no longer be expected to remain on the old estates. They moved instead in greater numbers to the cities where the wages were high. Those in the towns who survived the plague also profited financially. Geoffrey Chaucer's father, for example, lost many of his relatives but inherited a good deal of property.

People were also no longer confined to the social class into which they were born. The fourteenth century saw a lot of social mobility. The de la Pole family, for example, rose from Hull merchants to the earldom of Suffolk in two generations. Chaucer's own family went from tavern keepers to esquires at court in less than a hundred years. It is not surprising, therefore, that the questions of true 'gentility' should have interested Chaucer in *The Franklin's Prologue and Tale*.

However, all the changes in the social structure worried those who had always had power. Attempts were made to restore wages and conditions to pre-plague levels and it became an offence for men to seek new masters or higher wages. A poll (or head) tax was also introduced that demanded a shilling from every man and woman in the country, no matter how poor they were. The people grew discontented and then rebellious, resulting in the Peasants' Revolt of 1381.

Violence broke out in Essex and spread to Kent. The rebels marched on London, thousands of them pouring into the city at Aldgate, below Chaucer's house. Together with London workers they burned John of Gaunt's palace and stormed the Tower of London. The chancellor and the treasurer were killed, as were civil servants, lawyers and wealthy merchants. The violence was eventually brought under control but English society had changed.

The two great powers of the Middle Ages, the monarchy and the church, were also unstable. Richard II, only fourteen years old when he rode out to face the Peasants' Revolt, was deposed by his own noblemen as they struggled for power. He was forced from the throne by his cousin and died in prison in 1400. The church was no better. The papacy had moved from Rome to Avignon in the south of France in the early fourteenth century. In 1378, however, there was suddenly a rival pope set up in Rome. Two popes, both claiming the authority of God, competed for the loyalty of the people for nearly forty years. The church, like the monarchy, was in a state of conflict and confusion.

This then is the background to Chaucer's *Canterbury Tales*. It was a time of great change in which the status of many people was altered. A new class emerged consisting of merchants, physicians, cooks and businessmen. In the midst of this were the franklins, country gentlemen who were not quite noble enough to be part of the aristocracy but who were, nevertheless, part of the establishment, out making money and thriving under the new social order. They therefore straddled the old way of life and the new and this may be the reason for Chaucer's choice of tale for his Franklin: a lofty story of knights and ladies that tries to put forward a new way of living. The old feudal way of life had relied heavily on the swearing of oaths, upon noblemen being bound by their word of honour to serve their lord and showing unhesitating loyalty at all times. The fourteenth century, however, could no longer be sustained by these feudal ideals of lords and vassals joined in a common oath, and *The Franklin's Tale* both proves this and offers some sort of a way forward. Dorigen swears an oath that she will love Aurelius if he removes all the rocks from the sea and, as if they are living in feudal Britain, all the characters defy common sense and their natural inclinations and accept this oath as binding. They are paralysed by what they have sworn and caught in a world in which plighted troth will only result in misery all round. The way forward is to abandon such outdated feudal practices and focus instead on a new way of living that goes beyond the ancient oath. The answer is *gentillesse*, a much broader concept that demands good will, generosity and sound moral sense, not just from *gentle*men but from all ranks of society. The closing scenes of *The Franklin's Tale* show the characters competing to be just as *gentil* as the next man. It is not, of course, a complete success, especially as far as Dorigen is concerned, but it is a tale worthy of the more egalitarian fourteenth century. Some sort of equality for mankind can be advocated by the tale; equality for women is not yet possible.

LITERARY BACKGROUND

GENRE

The Franklin's Tale is a **romance**. Technically speaking it is a Breton **lai**, a subcategory of the genre that originated in France in the early Middle Ages. It is, in essence, a mini-romance that deals with one incident in a relatively short time, as opposed to full romances that are not just lengthy but can also follow the fortunes of knights through several generations and right across the globe. The Breton lai also tends to put a little more emphasis on magic. Its length and scope and liking for the magical are its distinguishing features, otherwise it has all the characteristics of a typical medieval romance. romances tend to be set long ago and often far away. They do not deal with the day-to-day lives of ordinary people but with the adventures of knights and their ladies. Concepts of honour and noble behaviour are of great importance to the romance writer. Knights are not required to have a lady but if they do they should treat her according to the rules of **courtly love**:

- The lover should regard himself as unworthy of his mistress and should live in constant fear of losing her or displeasing her in any way. His love should be kept secret at all times.

- The lover should present himself to his lady as her inferior, in a state of fear and trepidation. She should remain disdainful until his love has been proved.
- The lover should prove his worth by performing deeds of valour for his lady's sake. Her seeming 'harshness' is intended to spur him on and make him an even better man.
- Love should be regarded as an art, a science. It should be felt to be a strict code of which all the rules should be followed at all times.

This, then, is the genre Chaucer employs for *The Franklin's Prologue and Tale*. The genre is not, however, simply accepted. Instead, Chaucer adapts it for his purposes, playing with the notion of an ideal world with its supposed ideal way of life. He exploits the idea of romance heroines and courtly lovers and brings the whole tale into a far more realistic setting where concepts of love and honour are examined in a harsher light.

Sources

Telling a story that was new or original was not the most important thing in the Middle Ages. Many of the best-known authors adapted tales that had been around for hundreds of years, and this was not only accepted, it was encouraged. Authors who had in fact invented a whole new story often claimed that it was really an old one which they had heard somewhere. It is not to Chaucer's detriment, therefore, that he adapted his tale from the work of another author; the crucial thing is to note what changes he made to the plot, characters and themes of the original.

Boccaccio

The folk-tale of the 'Maiden's Rash Promise' is a very old one and exists in many cultures, the best known example perhaps being the tale of Rumpelstiltskin. Many different versions existed before Chaucer, but it appears that the source for *The Franklin's Tale* is *Il Filocolo*, one of the works of the medieval Italian writer, Giovanni Boccaccio:

A group of young noblemen and women are gathered together and are discussing various matters relating to the conduct of lovers. A young man named Menedon sets the others a puzzle, which he presents to them in the form of a story.

Once upon a time there lived a beautiful lady who was devoted to her husband. Her beauty, however, attracted the attention of a knight named Tarolfo who constantly tried to win her love, offering to do anything she commanded if she would only promise to love him. The lady grew tired of his petitions and thought of a way to rid herself of him. She said that she would indeed become his lover but only if he was able to create a May garden in the middle of January. The task seems impossible but Tarolfo journeys forth and eventually encounters an old man out gathering herbs. The old man's name is Tebano, and he claims that he is able to perform the task that will win the lady. A joyful Tarolfo promises the old man half his wealth and the two return to his land.

Tebano uses spells and herbs, gathered from across the globe, and succeeds in making the winter garden bloom. The lady is astonished but concedes that the knight has kept his part of the bargain and now she must keep hers. Sorrowfully, she tells her husband about her promise, saying that she would rather die than displease him or bring dishonour upon him. The husband tells her that she must keep her word and so she makes herself look beautiful and goes to meet Tarolfo. The sight of her there with all her attendants makes the knight realise that she must have told her husband and he asks her to explain. The lady tells him the whole story and Tarolfo has a change of heart: how can he bring dishonour to a man who has acted so nobly and generously? He sends the lady home unharmed. When Tebano hears what has happened he too wishes to be generous and refuses to accept the wealth that was promised to him for his services.

Menedon finishes his tale and the group discuss which of the characters was the most generous. The lady Fiammetta claims that the title must go to the husband because his honour was worth far more than the lust which Tarolfo gave up or the mere wealth which Tebano surrendered. Menedon answers that the opposite seems to be the case: the husband had no choice but to keep the bargain while both Tarolfo and Tebano had worked hard. Tarolfo has to give up his greatest desire while Tebano is perhaps even more generous, having now to return to a life of poverty. His case seems convincing but Fiammetta has not finished. The wife's promise, she claims, is invalidated by her earlier marriage vow to her husband. The husband is not, therefore, obliged to send her to Tarolfo. Similarly, if the oath was never valid in the first place, then Tarolfo cannot be called generous in setting it aside. He can only be generous with his lustful desires, and ridding himself of those, Fiammetta argues, cannot be called generosity. As for Tebano, a life of virtuous poverty is better than a life of wealth with all the problems that can bring. Thus, she concludes, the accolade must go to the husband.

The source story is, therefore, different from *The Franklin's Tale* in a number of respects. Most notably, it provides solutions where Chaucer chooses only to provide questions. *The Franklin's Tale* is not meant to be tied up so neatly at the end but is intended instead to leave readers unsettled, questioning what they have heard. Boccaccio's romance world is also replaced by a far more realistic fourteenth-century landscape in which Chaucer's experiment of equality in marriage can be played out. As for the characters, all Chaucer's characters display far more emotion. It is difficult to imagine Dorigen, for example, calmly prettifying herself before she goes off to meet Aurelius. Indeed, all the potential doubts about the wife's love for her husband are removed in Chaucer's version of the tale. This is reinforced by the task that Chaucer has Dorigen set. While one can imagine that it might be possible to get a garden somehow to bloom in January, Dorigen's task of having the rocks removed from the coast of Brittany is, rationally speaking, impossible. Any doubts we might have had about Dorigen's love for her husband are consequently swept away in this version of the tale and we can focus instead on the themes of *trouthe*, *gentillesse*, patience and the difficulties of marriage even between those who truly love one another.

BOETHIUS

Another source crucial to an understanding of *The Franklin's Prologue and Tale* is a work by the Roman philosopher Boethius. This work, the *De consolatione Philosophiae* (*Consolation of Philosophy*) was written in the early sixth century AD by a man about to be executed. Boethius had been a statesman and had been very powerful in Rome but his fortunes changed suddenly and he was tried for treason and sentenced to death. While in prison, he wrote the *Consolation*, a work in which a character named Boethius questions the way of the world, its apparent arbitrariness and injustice. This is perhaps not surprising for a man in his situation, but it is not just the lament of someone who felt he had been treated harshly. Boethius makes his complaints but he is answered by a character named Lady Philosophy who shows him that his complaints are not rational and that there is goodness and order in the world. Boethius himself was a Christian and in many ways his arguments are deeply Christian ones. However, his character in this work is a pagan who is led to consolation not by an easy appeal to God, but by reasoning and argument. Thus, although all the arguments he uses are compatible with Christianity, the comfort offered is available to everyone no matter what their religious beliefs.

The *Consolation of Philosophy* was very popular throughout the Middle Ages and Geoffrey Chaucer appears to have been particularly interested in it. Chaucer's *Boece* is his translation of this work into English but his fascination with the text did not end here and its ideas are to be found throughout his poetry. *The Franklin's Tale* is no exception. Boethian ideas are most prominent in Dorigen's lament about the rocks:

> Of swich a parfit wys God and a stable,
> Why han ye wroght this werk unresonable? …
> It dooth no good, to my wit, but anoyeth.
> Se ye nat, Lord, how mankinde it destroyeth?
> An hundred thousand bodies of mankinde
> Han rokkes slain, al be they nat in minde,
> Which mankinde is so fair part of thy werk
> That thou it madest lyk to thyn owene merk. (lines 199–208)

Looking down on the rocks and the surging sea Dorigen simply cannot understand how such forces could be at work in an ordered universe. It is a sentiment shared by the brooding Boethius as he considers his fate:

> O thou governour, governynge alle
> thynges by certein ende, whi refusestow oonly
> to governe the werkes of men by duwe manere?
> … We men, that ben noght a foul
> partie, but a fair partie of so greet a werk, we
> ben turmented in this see of fortune. Thow
> governour, withdraughe and restreyne the
> ravysschynge flodes. (*Boece*, I, metrum 5, ll.31–56)

[O governor, who rules all things according to a predetermined end, why do you refuse to govern the lives of men according to the rules? ... We men, who are not a foul part of your creation, but rather a beautiful part of it, are tormented in this sea of fortune. Lord, you must withdraw and hold back the violent floods]

The **metaphorical** floods of cruel fortune in Boethius become the dangerous sea to the more literal-minded Dorigen but the ideas are the same: both appeal to some ordering force in the universe, an idea of 'certain governaunce' (line 194), and ask how such a fair creation as man could be left to the mercy of such destructive forces. It is not an unfair question for Dorigen to ask and she is clearly keeping some illustrious company here. However, it does not mean that she is right. Boethius is led to an understanding that the world is benignly and carefully ruled, and in language that is very interesting in terms of *The Franklin's Tale*. He is instructed on the nature of cosmic love and is told by Lady Philosophy that all the potentially conflicting elements are held in place by everlasting law. Thus, Phoebus, the sun, rises every morning in his chariot, and the moon takes charge of the nights, and,

> [the] see, gredy to flowen, constreyneth with a
>
> certein eende his floodes, so that it is nat
>
> leveful to strecche his brode termes or
>
> bowndes uppon the erthes (that is to seyn, to
>
> coveren al the erthe ...) (*Boece*, II, metrum 8, ll.9–13)

[the sea, greedy to flow forth, is forced to hold back his waves within lawful bounds, and not permitted to extend his limits or boundaries onto the earth (that is to say, to completely cover the land)].

What is being described here is great goodness and order, an order that both Dorigen and Aurelius attempt to disrupt. The combination here of sun, moon and sea is reminiscent of Aurelius's first plan to cover the rocks as he prays to Phoebus Apollo and his sister Lucina, the moon, to transgress their usual boundaries and cause the sea to flood the earth (lines 359–98). It seems like a great plan to Aurelius, just as removing the rocks seems like an excellent idea to Dorigen, but they both have a flawed view of the world, for the very things they want to abolish are a **symbol** that all is, in fact, well. Only when it looks as though their prayers may be granted do they find themselves in any real danger.

The universe, according to Boethius, is held together by 'love, that governeth erthe and see' (*Boece*, II, metrum 8, l.15). It is a patient, enduring love that brings harmony to all aspects of existence:

> This love halt togideres peples joyned with an holy
> boond, and knytteth sacrement of mariages of
> chaste loves; and love enditeth lawes to trewe
> felawes. O weleful were mankynde, yif thilke
> love that governeth hevene governede yowr corages.
> (*Boece*, II, metrum 8, ll.21–6)

[Love binds together people joined by the holy bond of alliance, and unites chaste lovers in the sacrament of marriage; love makes the laws between true friends. O how happy the human race would be, if the love that rules heaven also ruled your hearts.]

But such patient, enduring, harmonious love is not what rules the hearts of Dorigen and Aurelius, who are instead intent on upsetting the order of things to their own detriment. They are not, however, just misguided pagans in a world they do not quite understand. Even Boethius needs a guide, a Lady Philosophy, to show him the way forward but no such teacher is available to the characters in *The Franklin's Prologue and Tale*. They learn some lessons on the way but are not technically provided with answers. Dorigen's lament on Providence as much as Aurelius's appeal to the pagan gods is met with silence, and although there is in fact order, even down to the careful structuring of the text itself (see Structure), the characters themselves do not share our privileged position. Thus, the end of the tale only sees the characters being placed back in their conventional roles.

PART SIX

CRITICAL HISTORY & FURTHER READING

There are many different critical responses and approaches to *The Franklin's Prologue and Tale*. The Franklin has been viewed as everything from a saintly philanthropist and representative of Chaucer himself, to a gluttonous, bad-tempered upstart and power-hungry villain. His tale too has been the focus of a great deal of critical debate. It has been heralded as forward thinking, naïve and reactionary, sometimes all three in one piece of criticism, for there is a great deal of ambiguity and doubt in this tale. In spite of this, criticism can be roughly divided into various schools of thought. Many critics do not fit easily into one group and many use a variety of arguments, but some basic categories still exist.

DRAMATIC THEORY

This way of viewing *The Canterbury Tales* was first proposed in the early twentieth century (Kittredge, 1915). The idea is that the tale and its teller should always be viewed together, because there is a lot that can be learned about the pilgrim character from the tale he or she tells and vice versa. This can result in readings such as Donald R. Howard's that the Franklin is just a simple country squire with a taste for courtly literature. This results in a tale of naïve optimism which shows 'aristocratic' characters backing down and making bargains, a conclusion that ultimately exposes the businessman who tells the tale (Howard, 1976). Other critics view the Franklin as nicely flawed, basically a solid character but with some aspirations that make him want to challenge the order of things. Dorigen and Arveragus do likewise and the result is a bit of a mess which the narrator is incapable of putting right (Burlin, 1974).

Critics in this category also look at the wider context of the tale to see if it is a response to any other pilgrim or part of a larger debate. The idea of a 'marriage group' of tales was popular for some time. According to this school of thought, marriage is a key theme in *The Canterbury Tales* and the Franklin's views on marriage are intended to be measured against three of the other tales: *The clerk's Tale* about a supremely patient and loyal wife; *The Merchant's Tale* about an old man and his faithless young wife; and *The Wife of Bath's Tale* about women's desire for sovereignty in marriage. The archetypal view on this is Kittredge's, that the Franklin does not just take part in the marriage debate, but offers the perfect solution, an ideal picture of love and marriage (Kittredge, 1915). Many other critics have adopted the 'marriage group' theory without necessarily accepting that the Franklin has the answer. However, the theory has become less popular in recent years. Most modern critics have felt that the four tales traditionally classed together as 'marriage tales' are not close enough to one another in the ordering of *The Canterbury Tales* as a whole for the theme to be meaningful, and that marriage is too vague a concept to hold them together anyway.

However, even without the 'marriage' connection, many critics still feel that the relationship between the tales is important (Cooper, 1989). Some believe that the matter can be extended to the much larger question of the relationship between sexuality and authority, and that this is an important theme for Chaucer throughout *The Canterbury Tales.*

Historical criticism

Just as the character of the Franklin is of crucial importance to the Dramatic Theorists, it has also been viewed in the light of much Historical Criticism. Such critics believe that knowledge about the history of the period can throw considerable light on the literature. Therefore, if we understand what it means to be a franklin in the fourteenth century, or how important the **courtly love** movement was, for instance, we shall have a better understanding of *The Franklin's Prologue and Tale.*

At one end of the spectrum this has involved looking for a real-life model for the character of the Franklin, but more popular has been the idea that Chaucer is not dealing with individuals at all but that he is instead portraying medieval types or 'estates'. This means that the Franklin should be viewed as the representative of the franklin class and is the object of Chaucer's **satire** about this social group (Mann, 1973).

There was a fashion for some time to believe that in presenting the Franklin, Chaucer was in fact condemning his type as upstart, *nouveaux riches* businessmen who were getting to the top with no understanding at all of how those in power should behave (Robertson, 1962). However, more recent criticism has moved more towards the view of the Franklin as a well-established country gentleman whose behaviour would not have been regarded as offensive (Specht, 1981).

NEW HISTORICISM & POLITICAL CRITICISM

The 1980s saw the rise of a slightly different kind of historicism, known as New Historicism. While history is still very important, this form of criticism does not attempt to place *The Franklin's Prologue and Tale* in any one historical context. History is interwoven with social, economic and political factors, though when the emphasis swings towards the last of these, what emerges is often called Political or Marxist Criticism. Such critics are not attempting to provide historical background information; they believe that literature cannot be separated from its broader cultural context. Some, for example, view the fourteenth century as a time when social boundaries were breaking down. Strohm (1989) in particular focuses on the idea of the oath of vassalage that was breaking down in Chaucer's time. He sees *The Franklin's Prologue and Tale* as showing the oath to be an outmoded concept and offering instead the idea of a world of good will where all men can perform noble deeds. For Aers (1980), on the other hand, the Franklin is enthusiastically presenting a **utopian** vision of equality that is colliding with the established male **patriarchy**. With so many social forces against him, says Aers, the Franklin cannot win but he does succeed in raising questions about the established order in the course of his tale.

FEMINIST CRITICISM

The focus of many critics on the social context of *The Franklin's Prologue and Tale* leads to a specific examination of the role of women in this world. Such criticism has revealed that both a feminist and a sexist reading can be supported by the tale. Martin (1990), for example, believes that Dorigen is ultimately excluded from the world of male power but, on her way from romance heroine to ordinary woman in the street, we do see her in relation to concepts such as *trouthe* and honour that are, for a while at least, not confined solely to the male world. A different perspective is offered by Hansen (1992) who regards *The Franklin's Tale* as an unambiguously **anti-feminist** text. In this interpretation, the lady of courtly love is seen as having too much power and a medieval wife cannot be allowed to act like this and must have her power removed upon marriage. Love is seen as reducing men to the level of women until they are able to overcome their desire and look instead for proper 'manly' virtues.

NEW CRITICISM

Of course, it is possible to read literature without any reference to the social or historical situation. According to **New Criticism**, knowledge of the Middle Ages is completely unnecessary for an understanding of *The Franklin's Prologue and Tale*. Such critics believe that all we need to know about the text is the text itself and that we can form an opinion about it simply by looking closely at the language Chaucer uses. This has led some critics to conclude that the Franklin is a 'Santa Claus' figure (Donaldson, 1975) but the opposite interpretation can equally be supported by other readings.

FURTHER READING

David Aers, *Chaucer, Langland and the Creative Imagination,* Routledge, 1980

> Prologue and tale as a **satire** of the social and economic situation

C. David Benson, *Chaucer's Drama of Style: Poetic Variety and Contrast in The Canterbury Tales,* University of North Carolina Press, 1986

> The tales interpreted in relation to their contrasting styles

Derek Brewer, *An Introduction to Chaucer*, Longman, 1984

> Society's demands and inner integrity in conflict. Personal integrity must prevail

Robert B. Burlin, 'The Art of Chaucer's Franklin', in *Chaucer, The Canterbury Tales: A Casebook*, Macmillan, 1974

> Franklin as a nicely flawed character with the desire to challenge the social order

Helen Cooper, *The Canterbury Tales*, Oxford University Press, 1989

> Introduction to the tales including sources and context. Many illusions in the tales, only the moral qualities are 'real'

E.T. Donaldson, *Chaucer's Poetry: An Anthology for the Modern Reader*, Ronald, New York, 1975

> A positive view of the Franklin in the light of New Criticism

Elaine Tuttle Hansen, *Chaucer and the Fictions of Gender*, University of California Press, 1992

> A feminist critique viewing the tale as re-establishing male power

Donald R. Howard, *The Idea of the Canterbury Tales*, University of California Press, 1976

> A tale of naïve optimism in which the aristocratic characters compromise and reveal Franklin to be a mere country squire

George Lyman Kittredge, *Chaucer and his Poetry*, Harvard University Press, 1915

> *The Franklin's Prologue and Tale* as offering the solution to the problems of the 'marriage group' of tales

R.M. Lumiansky, *Of Sondry Folk: The Dramatic Principle in the Canterbury Tales*, University of Texas Press, 1955

> Tale viewed in the context of its teller

Jill Mann, *Chaucer and Medieval Estates Satire: The Literature of Social Class and the General Prologue to the Canterbury Tales*, Cambridge University Press, 1973

> Chaucer's characters viewed in terms of their medieval 'estate' or type. A positive appraisal of the Franklin

Priscilla Martin, *Chaucer's Women: Nuns, Wives and Amazons*, Macmillan, 1990

An attempt by Chaucer to treat female virtues seriously

Derek Pearsall, *The Life of Geoffrey Chaucer*, Blackwell, 1992

Critical biography of Chaucer

Derek Pearsall, *The Canterbury Tales*, Allen and Unwin, 1985

Tale as a positive representation of a relationship of mutual tolerance

D. W. Robertson, *A Preface to Chaucer: Studies in Medieval Perspectives*, Princeton University Press, 1962

The Franklin as a social climber, unaware of how those in power should really behave

Henrik Specht, *Chaucer's Franklin in the Canterbury Tales: The Social and Literary Background of Chaucerian Character*, Akademisc Forlag, 1981

The Franklin and his tale as models of proper behaviour

Paul Strohm, *Social Chaucer*, Harvard University Press, 1989

Tale as an attempt to embrace the new social order

World events | Chaucer's life | Literary events

1300 Population of British Isles:
c. 5 million

1309 Papal See moves to Avignon and comes under French control

1313 Indulgences for public sale by Pope Clement V

1315 Death of Jean de Meun, author of part 2 of *Roman de la Rose*, allegorical poem mocking love, women, the Church and those in authority

1319 Death of Jean de Joinville, French chronicler

1321 Edward II forced to abdicate, imprisoned and probably murdered. Edward III accedes to throne, with wife Philippa

1321 Death of Dante Alighieri, author of *Divine Comedy*

1330 Birth of John Gower, friend of Chaucer and author

1331 Birth of William Langland, author

1337 Birth of Jean Froissart, who will become Clerk of the Chamber to Queen Philippa, and author of *Chronicles*, a brilliant history of 14th-century Europe

1338 Beginning of 100 Years War between France and England

1341 Petrarch crowned as laureate poet at Capitol, Rome

1343? Birth of **Geoffrey Chaucer** in London

1346 French routed at Crécy by Edward III and his son the Black Prince

World events	Chaucer's life	Literary events
1349 Black Death reaches England and kills one third of population		
1351 First Statute of Labourers regulates wages in England		
		1353 In Italy, Giovanni Boccaccio finishes his *Decameron*, a collection of 100 bawdy tales
	1357 Chaucer in service of Countess of Ulster, wife of Prince Lionel, 3rd son of Edward III	
1359 Edward III makes unsuccessful bid for French throne	**1359** Serves in army in France, under Prince Lionel; taken prisoner	
	1360 Edward III pays ransom of £16 for Chaucer's freedom	
1361 Black Death reappears in England		
1362 English becomes official language in Parliament and Law Courts		
		1363 Birth of Christine de Pisan, French author of *La Cité des Dames*, listing all the heroic acts and virtues of women
	1365 Marries Philippa Pan (or Payne) de Roet	
	1366 In Spain on diplomatic mission	
	1367 Granted life pension for his services to king; birth of his son Thomas	
	1368 On Prince Lionel's death, his services transferred to John of Gaunt, Duke of Lancaster	

World events	Chaucer's life	Literary events

1369 In France with John of Gaunt's expeditionary force; begins *Book of the Duchess* on death of Blanche, John of Gaunt's wife

1370-3 Sent on diplomatic missions (11 months in Italy)

1370 *(c.)* William Langland's *Piers Plowman*

1374 Appointed Controller of the Customs and Subsidy of Wools, Skins and Leather; receives life pension from John of Gaunt

1375 *(c.) Sir Gawain and the Green Knight* written

1376 Receives payment for some secret, unspecified service

1377 Edward III dies and is succeeded by Richard II, son of the Black Prince

1377 Employed on secret missions to Flanders, and sent to France to negotiate for peace with Charles V; employed on further missions in France, Lombardy and Italy

1378 Beginning of the Great Schism: Urban VI elected Pope in Rome, Clement VII in Avignon

1380 John Wyclif, who attacked orthodox Church doctrines, condemned as heretic. Wyclif's followers translate Bible into vernacular

1380 *Parliament of Fowls* written; birth of son Lewis. Cecilia Chaumpayne releases Chaucer from charge of '*de raptu meo*'

1381 Peasant's Revolt under Wat Tyler quelled by Richard II

World events	Chaucer's life	Literary events
	1382 Appointed, in addition, Controller of the Petty Customs	
	1385 Allowed privilege of appointing deputy to perform his duties as Controller. Probably writes *Legend of Good Women* and *Troilus and Criseyde*	
	1385-99 Now living in Greenwich	
1386 Richard II deprived of power	**1386** Deprived of both official posts. Elected Knight of Shire of Kent	
	1387 Wife Philippa dies. Begins writing *The Canterbury Tales*	
	1388 In poverty, Chaucer sells his pensions to raise money	
1389 Richard II resumes power	**1389** Appointed clerk of king's works at Westminster	**1389** John Gower completes first version of *Confessio Amantis*
	1391 Writes *Treatise on the Astrolabe* for his son Lewis. Resigns as clerk of king's works and becomes deputy forester of royal forest at North Petherton, Somerset	
1396 John of Gaunt marries his mistress, Katherine (de Roet), Chaucer's sister-in-law		
1399 Richard II forced to abdicate. Henry IV becomes King of England		
1400 Richard II dies in prison. Population of British Isles *c*. 3.5 million	**1400** Chaucer dies	
		1450 Gutenberg produces first printed book in moveable type

ambiguous referring to the capacity of words and sentences to have double, multiple or uncertain meanings

anti-feminist literature medieval literature which criticises women

Chaucerian irony see irony

couplet a pair of rhymed lines

courtly love love conducted according to a system of high chivalric ideals (see Background, on Medieval Marriage & Courtly Love)

dramatic theory a method of literary criticism in which the tale and the teller are always viewed together

feminism referring to the numerous different approaches involved in investigating the subordination of women in patriarchal society, i.e. man-centred society based upon 'the law of the father'

historical criticism a method of literary criticism, based on Historicism, in which the text is viewed in the light of its particular historical context

image, imagery language referring to objects and qualities which evoke a particular emotion or feeling

irony saying one thing but meaning something else. **Chaucerian irony** using exuberant praise to undermine a character

lai short narrative poem which originated in France. Poems written in the fourteenth century concerning Celtic legends were called 'Breton lais'

metaphor a comparison in which something is said to 'be' something else

New Criticism a type of literary criticism which concentrates solely on the text and the language used, and ignores the social and historical contexts in which it was written

New Historicism the text is viewed in the light of not just one historical context, but also social, economic and political factors. Critics believe that literature cannot be separated from its broader cultural background

paradox an apparently self-contradictory statement

patriarchy see feminism

rhetoric the art of persuasive speech or writing

romance medieval prose or verse dealing with adventures of chivalry and courtly love

satire literature that exposes wickedness or folly and makes them appear ridiculous

simile a comparison in which something is said to be 'like' something else

stereotype stock characters, ideas and situations that are the typical material of literature

symbol something which represents something else, often an idea or quality, by analogy or association

synonym a word with a meaning identical to that of another word

utopian fictional, philosophical or political works that depict imaginary worlds better than our own

Author of this note

J.A. Tasioulas is a Fellow in English at Newnham College, Cambridge. She received her M.A. in English Language and Literature from the University of Glasgow and became a Snell Exhibitioner to Balliol College, Oxford where she obtained a D.Phil in medieval English. She was formerly a Junior Fellow at New College, Oxford and a Lecturer in English Studies at the University of Stirling. She has published on various aspects of medieval literature and culture, including an Advanced York Note on Chaucer's *The Wife of Bath's Prologue and Tale*. She is the editor of *The Makars: The Poems of Henryson, Dunbar and Douglas* (Canongate Press, 1999).

Chinua Achebe
Things Fall Apart

Edward Albee
Who's Afraid of Virginia Woolf?

Jane Austen
Emma

Jane Austen
Northanger Abbey

Jane Austen
Sense and Sensibility

Samuel Beckett
Waiting for Godot and *Endgame*

Louis de Bernières
Captain Corelli's Mandolin

Charlotte Brontë
Villette

Robert Browning
Selected Poems

Robert Burns
Selected Poems

Geoffrey Chaucer
The Merchant's Tale

Geoffrey Chaucer
The Nun's Priest's Tale

Caryl Churchill
Top Girls and *Cloud Nine*

Samuel Taylor Coleridge
Selected Poems

Daniel Defoe
Moll Flanders

Daniel Defoe
Robinson Crusoe

Charles Dickens
Bleak House

T.S. Eliot
The Waste Land

Henry Fielding
Joseph Andrews

E.M. Forster
Howards End

John Fowles
The French Lieutenant's Woman

Anne Frank
The Diary of Anne Frank

Robert Frost
Selected Poems

Elizabeth Gaskell
North and South

Stella Gibbons
Cold Comfort Farm

Graham Greene
Brighton Rock

Thomas Hardy
Jude the Obscure

Joseph Heller
Catch-22

Homer
The Iliad

Homer
The Odyssey

Gerard Manley Hopkins
Selected Poems

Henrik Ibsen
The Doll's House and *Ghosts*

Ben Jonson
The Alchemist

Ben Jonson
Volpone

James Joyce
A Portrait of the Artist as a Young Man

Philip Larkin
Selected Poems

Aldous Huxley
Brave New World

D.H. Lawrence
The Rainbow

D.H. Lawrence
Selected Poems

D.H. Lawrence
Selected Stories

D.H. Lawrence
Sons and Lovers

D.H. Lawrence
Women in Love

Christopher Marlowe
Edward II

John Milton
Paradise Lost Bks IV & IX

Thomas More
Utopia

Sean O'Casey
Juno and the Paycock

George Orwell
Nineteen Eighty-four

John Osborne
Look Back in Anger

Wilfred Owen
Selected Poems

Sylvia Plath
Selected Poems

Alexander Pope
Rape of the Lock and other poems

Ruth Prawer Jhabvala
Heat and Dust

J.B. Priestley
When We Are Married

Jean Rhys
Wide Sargasso Sea

William Shakespeare
As You Like It

William Shakespeare
Coriolanus

William Shakespeare
Henry IV Pt I

Wliiam Shakespeare
Henry IV Part II

William Shakespeare
Henry V

William Shakespeare
Julius Caesar

William Shakespeare
Macbeth

William Shakespeare
Measure for Measure

William Shakespeare
Richard III

William Shakespeare
Sonnets

William Shakespeare
Twelfth Night

William Shakespeare
The Winter's Tale

George Bernard Shaw
Arms and the Man

Muriel Spark
The Prime of Miss Jean Brodie

John Steinbeck
The Grapes of Wrath

John Steinbeck
The Pearl

FUTURE TITLES (continued)

Tom Stoppard
Arcadia and *Rosencrantz and Guildenstern are Dead*

Jonathan Swift
Gulliver's Travels and The Modest Proposal

Alfred, Lord Tennyson
Selected Poems

W.M. Thackeray
Vanity Fair

Virgil
The Aeneid

Edith Wharton
Ethan Frome

Jeanette Winterson
Oranges are Not the Only Fruit and *Written on the Body*

Tennessee Williams
Cat on a Hot Tin Roof

Tennessee Williams
The Glass Menagerie

Virginia Woolf
Mrs Dalloway

William Wordsworth
Selected Poems

The Diary of Anne Frank

Metaphysical Poets